Hamlyn all-colour cookbooks

Dinner and Supper Parties

Marguerite Patten

Hamlyn
London · New York · Sydney · Toronto

Published by
The Hamlyn Publishing Group Limited
London · New York · Sydney · Toronto
Astronaut House, Feltham, Middlesex, England
© Copyright The Hamlyn Publishing Group Limited 1973
First published 1973
Reprinted 1974
ISBN 0 600 30211 3
Printed in England by Sir Joseph Causton and Sons Limited
Line drawings by John Scott Martin
Set 'Monophoto' by Page Bros (Norwich) Limited

Contents

Useful facts and figures

Note on metrication

In this book quantities are given in both Imperial and metric measures. Exact conversion from Imperial to metric does not always give very convenient working quantities so for greater convenience and ease of working we have taken an equivalent of 25 grammes/millilitres to the ounce/fluid ounce. 1 oz. is exactly 28·35 g. and $\frac{1}{4}$ pint (5 fl. oz.) is 142 ml., so you will see that by using the unit of 25 you will get a slightly smaller result than the Imperial measures would give.

Occasionally, for example in a basic recipe such as a Victoria sandwich made with 4 oz. flour, butter and sugar and 2 eggs, we have rounded the conversion up to give a more generous result. For larger amounts where the exact conversion is not critical, for instance in soups or stews, we have used kilogrammes and fractions (1 kg. equals 2·2 lb.) and litres and fractions (1 litre equals 1·76 pints). All recipes have been individually converted so that each recipe preserves the correct proportions.

Oven temperatures

The following chart gives the Celsius (Centigrade) equivalents recommended by the Electricity Council.

Description	Fahrenheit	Celsius	Gas Mark
Very cool	225	110	$\frac{1}{4}$
	250	130	$\frac{1}{2}$
Cool	275	140	1
	300	150	2
Moderate	325	170	3
	350	180	4
Moderately hot	375	190	5
	400	200	6
Hot	425	220	7
	450	230	8
Very hot	475	240	9

Introduction

Most of us enjoy issuing invitations to our friends and acquaintances to join us for dinner or supper. An occasion like this enables everyone to have a relaxed celebration meal. I hope that the recipes in this book will encourage the hostess (or the host, if he does the cooking) to feel almost as relaxed as the guests, for while they are all 'special-occasion' dishes, they are not too difficult or time-consuming to prepare.

The first part of the book deals with interesting starters, for example, salads and egg dishes. This is followed by fish dishes, which you may care to serve as a light main dish or as an hors d'oeuvre. The main dishes, using meats of various kinds, range from a Chinese inspired sweet and sour pork (page 72) and a delicious way of cooking tongue (page 54) to more familiar ideas for cooking joints, steaks or chops. The desserts are to be found from page 94 onwards. While I have tried to give you unusual recipes I have concentrated on the kind of dishes you can prepare beforehand.

When you plan your special menu choose the main dish first; this will then enable you to select a starter and a dessert which will form pleasing contrasts in colour, texture and flavour to the main course. I hope you will find this book helpful and that it will enable you to plan many happy dinner and supper parties.

Interesting dips

A savoury dip makes an excellent celebration dish. It can be served with a variety of foods, e.g., potato crisps, small biscuits, tiny carrots, pieces of celery, raw cauliflower. Quantities below make a good-sized bowlful which will serve about 8.

Commercial flavourings for dips: It is possible to buy excellent dehydrated flavourings for dips, e.g., green onion, etc., and these can be blended with a cottage cheese dip, as below, to give a different flavour. Following the directions on the packet, add the dip flavouring to the recipes below.

Cottage cheese dip
Blend 12 oz. (300 g.) cottage cheese with $\frac{1}{4}$ pint (125 ml.) dairy soured cream, 3–4 tablespoons mayonnaise and the dip flavouring. If you find the mixture a little too thick, blend in a little extra cream or mayonnaise; add a little brandy or sherry to taste.

Cheddar cheese dip
Grate 1 lb. ($\frac{1}{2}$ kg.) Cheddar cheese, blend with $\frac{1}{4}$ pint (150 ml.) thick and $\frac{1}{4}$ pint (150 ml.) thin cream, seasoning, 3 tablespoons diced gherkins and 3 tablespoons chopped olives. Dip flavourings may be added if wished. A little port gives an excellent flavour.

Avocado and cheese dip
Use either of the previous recipes and add the pulp from 1 large ripe avocado pear. Do not cut the pear until ready to use as the flesh discolours easily. The dip flavourings may also be added if wished.

Crab and cheese dip
Add a medium-sized can of crab meat or the meat from a medium-sized cooked crab to either of the basic recipes. The meat should be flaked finely and mixed well so it is smooth and creamy. The dip flavourings may also be added if wished.

Lobster chowder

Cooking time: 30 minutes
Preparation time: 15 minutes
Main cooking utensils: large saucepan, frying pan
Serves: 4–6

Imperial	Metric
1 medium-sized cooked lobster	1 medium-sized cooked lobster
1 pint water	550 ml. water
1–2 rashers bacon	1–2 rashers bacon
tiny onion	tiny onion
1½ oz. flour	40 g. flour
1 medium-sized potato	1 medium-sized potato
generous ¼ pint top of milk or single cream	150 ml. top of milk or single cream
seasoning	seasoning
pinch sugar	pinch sugar
chopped parsley	chopped parsley

1. Remove all the flesh from the lobster.

2. Simmer the shell in the water for 15 minutes, then strain and add to the resulting liquid enough water to make up to 1 pint (550 ml.) again.

3. Fry the chopped bacon and chopped onion for a few minutes then sprinkle over the flour. Stir in the lobster stock and bring to the boil, stirring until thickened.

4. Add the diced potato, lobster meat, seasoning and sugar and heat gently for 10 minutes.

5. Serve hot, sprinkled with chopped parsley, with croûtons or French bread.

Variation

Hamburger chowder: Heat a can of oxtail soup and add 4 oz. (100 g.) cooked minced beef, some cooked diced vegetables, and a little cooked rice. Heat for a few minutes and serve sprinkled with parsley.

Melon and raspberry coronet

Preparation time: 10–15 minutes
Main utensils: vegetable scoop, sharp knife
Serves: 4

Imperial	Metric
1 medium-sized ripe melon (see note)	1 medium-sized ripe melon (see note)
approximately 8 oz. fresh or well-drained canned raspberries	approximately 200 g. fresh or well-drained canned raspberries
sugar	sugar
little sherry (optional)	little sherry (optional)

1. Remove the top from the melon in a zig-zag fashion. To do this, make a cut with a sharp knife downwards, then cut up, then down again all the way round the fruit, feeling the point of the knife going through the flesh. Remove the slice from the top.
2. Take out the seeds, then cut out the centre pulp.
3. To make balls, insert the vegetable scoop into the flesh and turn it slowly and carefully. In this way you cut out a neat complete ball.
4. Mix with the raspberries, adding a little sugar with fresh fruit and sherry if wished.
5. Pile back again into the melon case.
6. Serve as cold as possible.

Note: There are various types of melon. Cantaloup and Charentais are the most usual and best. Watermelon has an individual flavour with bright red flesh. Ogen or Charentais melons are small fruit which are halved to serve — each person having half a melon.

Variation
This may be served as a sweet; or omit the raspberries and serve the melon with sugar and ginger.

Prawn and grape cocktail

Preparation time: 10 minutes
Main utensils: 4 sundae glasses or small dishes
Serves: 4

Imperial	Metric
small lettuce	small lettuce
2–3 tomatoes	2–3 tomatoes
$\frac{1}{4}$ pint mayonnaise	125 ml. mayonnaise
2–3 tablespoons fruit-flavoured bottled sauce	2–3 tablespoons fruit-flavoured bottled sauce
small bunch green grapes	small bunch green grapes
6 oz. shelled prawns (see note)	150 g. shelled prawns (see note)
Garnish:	*Garnish:*
2 fairly thick slices lemon	2 fairly thick slices lemon
sprigs parsley	sprigs parsley

1. Wash the lettuce, shake dry and shred finely; this is important as the cocktails are served with a small teaspoon and small fork and the lettuce is very difficult to manage if it is in large pieces.
2. Cut the tomatoes into wafer-thin slices; choose tomatoes that are not too large.
3. Blend the mayonnaise and the sauce, adding enough of the latter to give a pleasant 'bite' to the mixture.
4. Slit the grapes carefully and remove any seeds with the tip of a sharp knife.
5. Put the lettuce and tomatoes into the glasses and top with some of the dressing.
6. Add the grapes and prawns and more dressing.
7. Halve the lemon slices and top each cocktail with half a lemon slice and parsley.

Note: If using frozen prawns allow to defrost at room temperature. To hasten the process put the packet of frozen prawns in cold water — NOT hot.

Variation
Use diced melon or grapefruit segments instead of grapes.

Jamaican prawn hors d'oeuvre

Preparation time: 15 minutes
Serves: 4

Imperial	Metric
16 prawns or 8–12 oz. small shrimps, chopped	16 prawns or 200–300 g. small shrimps, chopped
1 red chilli pepper, chopped	1 red chilli pepper, chopped
grated rind and juice of 1 lemon	grated rind and juice of 1 lemon
1 tablespoon olive oil	1 tablespoon olive oil
seasoning	seasoning
1 clove garlic, crushed	1 clove garlic, crushed
1 lettuce	1 lettuce
Garnish:	*Garnish:*
8 whole prawns	8 whole prawns

1. Shell the prawns, devein them and chop finely.

2. Mix with the chopped chilli pepper, lemon rind and juice, olive oil, seasoning and garlic.

3. Wash and dry the lettuce.

4. To serve, place a bed of lettuce on individual serving dishes and spoon the prawn mixture over. Serve with bread and butter or biscuits.

Avocado dressing for shellfish

Put the flesh of an avocado into a bowl and mash until smooth with the juice of a medium-sized lemon, 1 teaspoon olive oil, 1 teaspoon made mustard and 2–3 tablespoons mayonnaise. Season with chilli powder, cayenne pepper, a few drops Tabasco sauce and salt. Serve with prepared fish or shellfish.

Fish in pastry shells

Cooking time: 20 minutes
Preparation time: 30 minutes
Main cooking utensils: patty tins or scallop shell tins, saucepan
Oven temperature: hot (425–450°F., 220–230°C., Gas Mark 7–8)
Oven position: above centre
Serves: 6–8

Imperial	Metric
8 oz. shortcrust pastry (see page 23)	200 g. shortcrust pastry (see page 23)
Filling:	*Filling:*
2 oz. butter	50 g. butter
2 oz. mushrooms	50 g. mushrooms
$\frac{1}{2}$ oz. potato flour or cornflour	15 g. potato flour or cornflour
2 teaspoons curry powder	2 teaspoons curry powder
2 tablespoons chutney	2 tablespoons chutney
$\frac{1}{4}$ pint fish stock or white stock	125 ml. fish stock or white stock
seasoning	seasoning
8–10 oz. cooked but firm white fish	200–250 g. cooked but firm white fish
approximately $\frac{1}{2}$ pint unshelled prawns or 2 oz. shelled prawns	approximately $\frac{1}{4}$ litre unshelled prawns or 50 g. shelled prawns
Garnish:	*Garnish:*
parsley	parsley
few prawns	few prawns

1. Make and roll out the pastry, line the patty or scallop shell tins.
2. Bake blind until crisp and brown. Alternatively, use ready-made cases and heat through.
3. Heat the butter and fry the sliced mushrooms in it until tender.
4. Stir in the potato flour or cornflour, and cook for several minutes.
5. Add the curry powder, chutney and stock, bring to the boil and season.
6. Cook until smooth and clear.
7. Add the flaked cooked white fish, simmer for a few minutes then add most of the prawns, shelled.
8. Pile the hot fish mixture into the hot pastry cases, garnish with parsley and a few unshelled prawns.

Variation

Make a sauce from 2 oz. (50 g.) butter, 1 oz. (25 g.) flour, seasoning, 12 tablespoons milk and 5 tablespoons cream. Heat the cooked fish in this and add cooked peas or other vegetables. Use chopped dill pickles instead of chutney.

Shellfish ring

Cooking time: 20 minutes
Preparation time: 30 minutes
Main cooking utensils: 2 saucepans, 8- to 9-inch (20- to 23-cm.)
  ring mould
Serves: 8

Imperial	Metric
Ring:	*Ring:*
1½–2 lb. white fish (free from skin and bone)	¾–1 kg. white fish (free from skin and bone)
seasoning	seasoning
2 oz. butter	50 g. butter
2 oz. flour	50 g. flour
½ pint milk	250 ml. milk
½ pint fish stock	250 ml. fish stock
3 tablespoons dry sherry or lemon juice	3 tablespoons dry sherry or lemon juice
¾ oz. powder gelatine	20 g. powder gelatine
½ pint thick cream	250 ml. thick cream
very little oil	very little oil
Filling:	*Filling:*
2 pints large, unshelled prawns	1¼ litres large, unshelled prawns
¼ pint mayonnaise	125 ml. mayonnaise
¼ pint thick cream, lightly whipped	125 ml. thick cream, lightly whipped
few drops Worcestershire sauce	few drops Worcestershire sauce
juice of 1 lemon	juice of 1 lemon
3 tablespoons tomato ketchup or sieved pulp of fresh tomatoes	3 tablespoons tomato ketchup or sieved pulp of fresh tomatoes

1. Put the fish with just enough water to cover and seasoning into a pan. Bring to the boil, simmer for approximately 5 minutes only.

2. Remove the fish from the pan and reserve the stock.

3. Flake and pound the fish until it is very smooth; strain the fish stock.

4. Heat the butter in a pan, add the flour, cook for 2–3 minutes, then gradually blend in the milk and ½ pint (250 ml.) of the fish stock.

5. Bring to the boil, cook until thickened.

6. Blend the sherry with the gelatine in a basin over a pan of hot water until dissolved, stir into the hot sauce.

7. Add the fish, allow to cool and begin to thicken, fold in the lightly whipped cream.

8. Brush the mould with oil, spoon in the fish mixture, leave to set.

9. Shell the prawns, stir into a dressing made by blending all the remaining ingredients together.

10. Put the prawn mixture into the fish ring, serve as cold as possible.

Eggs with vegetables

Cooking time: 20 minutes
Preparation time: 35 minutes
Main cooking utensils: patty tins, 3 saucepans
Oven temperature: hot (425–450°F., 220–230°C., Gas Mark 7–8)
Oven position: above centre
Serves: 6

Imperial	Metric
Shortcrust pastry:	*Shortcrust pastry:*
8 oz. plain flour	200 g. plain flour
pinch salt	pinch salt
4 oz. butter	100 g. butter
water to mix	water to mix
Filling:	*Filling:*
8 oz. spinach or a small packet frozen spinach	200 g. spinach or a small packet frozen spinach
seasoning	seasoning
1 oz. butter	25 g. butter
¼ pint thin cream	125 ml. thin cream
small amount fresh asparagus or small can asparagus tips	small amount fresh asparagus or small can asparagus tips
1 large potato	1 large potato
1 large carrot	1 large carrot
6 eggs	6 eggs
Garnish:	*Garnish:*
paprika pepper	paprika pepper

1. Sieve the flour and salt, rub in the butter and bind with a little water, roll out and line some fairly deep patty tins.
2. Bake blind until crisp and brown.
3. Cook the spinach until tender without water (or as directed on the packet of frozen spinach), season well, drain and chop or sieve to give a smooth mixture.
4. Reheat with butter and cream.
5. Meanwhile cook or heat the asparagus, cook the diced potato and carrot.
6. Drain and mix with the spinach cream.
7. Poach the eggs in salted water, drain very thoroughly.
8. Put the hot vegetable mixture into the hot pastry cases, top with the eggs and sprinkle with the pepper. Serve as soon as possible after filling.

Variation
Omit the pastry shells and serve in small individual cocotte dishes with Melba toast. Other combinations of vegetables may be used, but you need to include butter and cream for a moist texture.

Spanish omelette with peppers

Cooking time: 15 minutes
Preparation time: 10 minutes
Main cooking utensils: frying pan, omelette pan
Serves: 6–8 as an hors d'oeuvre, 4 people as a main dish

Imperial	Metric
2 cloves garlic (optional)	2 cloves garlic (optional)
1 large onion	1 large onion
8 large tomatoes	8 large tomatoes
2 large or 4 smaller green peppers	2 large or 4 smaller green peppers
4 tablespoons oil	4 tablespoons oil
seasoning	seasoning
Omelettes:	*Omelettes:*
8 large or 10 medium eggs	8 large or 10 medium eggs
seasoning	seasoning
3 oz. butter or 3 tablespoons oil	75 g. butter or 3 tablespoons oil

1. Crush the cloves of garlic very finely. (Put the skinned clove on a board with a good pinch of salt, crush with the tip of a strong knife.)

2. Chop the onion very finely; skin the tomatoes.

3. Cut the flesh from the green and red peppers into strips, discard the core and seeds.

4. Heat the oil in the pan, fry the vegetables until they are as soft as wished; some people prefer the peppers to be firm, so add these when the onion and tomatoes are nearly soft. If wished, blanch the peppers for a softer texture (see note). Season well.

5. Beat the eggs with seasoning; for a slightly lighter, less rich omelette, add 2—4 tablespoons water.

6. Heat half the butter or oil in an omelette pan, pour in half the egg mixture, allow to set on the bottom, then tilt the pan to allow the liquid egg on top to flow down the sides.

7. When lightly set, tip on to a serving dish; do not fold. Make the second omelette. Serve topped with the very hot vegetable mixture.

Note: Peppers may be simmered for about 5—10 minutes in salted water to give a softened texture.

Potato and ham mould

Cooking time: 40–45 minutes
Preparation time: 20 minutes
Main cooking utensils: saucepan, ovenproof plate or dish
Oven temperature: moderate (375°F., 190°C., Gas Mark 5)
Oven position: centre
Serves: 6

Imperial	Metric
1½–2 lb. potatoes (weight when peeled)	¾–1 kg. potatoes (weight when peeled)
2 oz. butter or margarine	50 g. butter or margarine
seasoning	seasoning
8 oz. finely grated cheese (Mozzarella or Cheddar)	300 g. finely grated cheese (Mozzarella or Cheddar)
2 eggs	2 eggs
little flour (optional, see stage 3)	little flour (optional, see stage 3)
6–8 oz. thinly sliced prosciutto (see note)	150–200 g. thinly sliced prosciutto (see note)
3–4 tablespoons thick cream	3–4 tablespoons thick cream
½ tomato	½ tomato

1. Cook the potatoes steadily so that they become evenly soft, strain, return to the pan and 'dry out' over a low heat.

2. Mash or sieve, beat in the butter, seasoning and 6 oz. (150 g.) finely grated cheese, do not add any milk.

3. Beat in the eggs and a little flour if the mixture seems too soft; this is better omitted and should not be necessary.

4. Put on to a lightly floured board, roll gently with a floured rolling pin and divide into three round portions, or pat out into three rounds. The rounds can be the same size or becoming slightly smaller to form a pyramid shape.

5. Put the first round on to an ovenproof plate, top with the chosen meat, cover with the second round and continue the layers, finishing with a layer of meat.

6. Beat together the remaining cheese, seasoning and cream, spread this over the meat and top with a halved tomato.

7. Bake until hot, do not overcook.

Note: Prosciutto is the Italian smoked, raw Parma ham, very much cheaper in Italy than in other countries, where it is a luxurious delicacy. You can substitute cheap pieces of cooked ham, salami, cooked sausage or grilled bacon.

American crab salad

Preparation time: 15 minutes
Serves: 6–8

Imperial	Metric
2 large or 4 medium-sized crabs	2 large or 4 medium-sized crabs
$\frac{1}{4}$ cucumber	$\frac{1}{4}$ cucumber
2 apples	2 apples
$\frac{1}{4}$ pint mayonnaise	125 ml. mayonnaise
grated rind and juice of 1 lemon	grated rind and juice of 1 lemon
black pepper	black pepper
Garnish:	*Garnish:*
sliced cucumber	sliced cucumber

1. Pull the claws from the crabs, crack them and remove the meat. Open the body shell, remove the inedible stomach bag and the grey fingers where the smaller claws join the body.
2. Peel and dice the cucumber and mix with the crab meat.
3. Core and dice the apples; if they are a good colour do not peel them. Blend the apples with the cucumber and crab meat and mix in the mayonnaise, lemon rind and juice and a sprinkling of black pepper.
4. Serve in a shallow dish, topped with sliced cucumber, with a green or mixed salad. This dish is ideal for a buffet party.

Crab ramekins

Prepare 1 large or 2 medium-sized crabs as above. Heat 2 oz. (50 g.) butter, fry a small chopped onion and 4 oz. (100 g.) sliced mushrooms. Blend in 1 oz. (25 g.) flour, cook for several minutes, add $\frac{1}{2}$ pint (250 ml.) milk, bring to the boil and cook until thickened. Season well, add 4 medium-sized, cooked, diced potatoes and flaked crab meat. Put into 4 individual dishes, top with 2 oz. (50 g.) breadcrumbs mixed with 2 oz. (50 g.) melted butter. Bake for about 15 minutes in a moderately hot oven (400°F., 200°C., Gas Mark 6) until crisp and golden.

Mussels with cheese

Cooking time: 20 minutes
Preparation time: 20 minutes
Main cooking utensils: large saucepan, ovenproof dish
Serves: 4–6

Imperial	Metric
2 pints mussels	a generous litre mussels
1 onion	1 onion
6 sticks celery	6 sticks celery
salt	salt
8 oz. tomatoes	200 g. tomatoes
4 oz. Gouda cheese	100 g. Gouda cheese
Garnish:	*Garnish:*
parsley	parsley

1. Clean the mussels in cold water and remove the black weed. Discard any that will not close when tapped sharply.
2. Place the mussels in a pan with the chopped onion, celery and salt.
3. Cover, bring to the boil and simmer until all the shells are open.
4. Remove from the heat and drain. When cool remove the mussels from the shells and discard half the shells.
5. Skin the tomatoes, remove the pips and chop the fleshy part finely.
6. Place each mussel in one half of a shell and arrange on a dish.
7. Blend the chopped tomatoes, seasoning and finely grated cheese.
8. Spread the tomato mixture over the mussels.
9. Brown under the grill and garnish with parsley. Serve hot as an hors d'oeuvre or light supper dish with a green salad.

Variations
Canned mussels could be used; heat, then drain and put in a dish, top with the tomato mixture and brown under the grill. Another way of serving the ingredients above is to omit the onions and celery when cooking the mussels. Then fry the celery and onions with an extra onion. Put this cooked vegetable purée with tomatoes on to the mussels, then add the cheese and brown under the grill.

Devilled lobster

Cooking time: few minutes plus time to cook the lobsters
Preparation time: 10 minutes
Main cooking utensils: large saucepan, grill pan
Serves: 4

Imperial	Metric
2 medium-sized lobsters	2 medium-sized lobsters
2 oz. butter	50 g. butter
1 clove garlic (optional)	1 clove garlic (optional)
2 teaspoons curry powder	2 teaspoons curry powder
shake cayenne pepper	shake cayenne pepper
Sauce:	*Sauce:*
2 egg yolks	2 egg yolks
1–2 teaspoons French mustard	1–2 teaspoons French mustard
1 teaspoon curry powder	1 teaspoon curry powder
shake cayenne pepper	shake cayenne pepper
pinch salt	pinch salt
pinch sugar	pinch sugar
up to $\frac{1}{2}$ pint olive oil	up to 275 ml. olive oil
1 tablespoon lemon juice	1 tablespoon lemon juice
2 teaspoons finely chopped tarragon	2 teaspoons finely chopped tarragon
Garnish:	*Garnish:*
lettuce	lettuce

1. If the lobsters are alive, tie the claws firmly. Put them into a pan of cold water and bring the water slowly to the boil, or plunge them into boiling water.

2. Boil steadily until the shells turn scarlet (about 15–20 minutes), allow to cool. Alternatively, buy cooked lobsters.

3. Split the lobsters down the centre and remove the intestinal veins (the long thread-like vein in the body); also discard the 'lady fingers' (the grey fingers that are found where the claws join the body).

4. If wished, the large claws may be used in a separate dish or crack these, remove the flesh and put this into the body of the lobsters.

5. Cream the butter with the crushed garlic, curry powder and cayenne and spread over the lobsters. Heat under the grill.

6. To make the curry sauce, blend the egg yolks with the seasoning and sugar, very gradually blend in the oil, lemon juice and herbs. Garnish with lettuce.

Freshwater shellfish with sauce

Cooking time: 10 minutes
Preparation time: few minutes
Main cooking utensil: saucepan
Serves: 4

Imperial	Metric
8–12 crayfish (see note)	8–12 crayfish (see note)
water	water
1 teaspoon salt	1 teaspoon salt
1 teaspoon vinegar	1 teaspoon vinegar
1 lettuce	1 lettuce
little chopped dill	little chopped dill
few nasturtium leaves	few nasturtium leaves
Cold dill sauce:	*Cold dill sauce:*
1–2 teaspoons dry mustard	1–2 teaspoons dry mustard
1 tablespoon sugar	1 tablespoon sugar
1 teaspoon salt	1 teaspoon salt
good shake cayenne pepper	good shake cayenne pepper
6 tablespoons olive oil	6 tablespoons olive oil
3 tablespoons white wine or malt vinegar or lemon juice	3 tablespoons white wine or malt vinegar or lemon juice

1. Wash the crayfish and either put them into cold water with the salt and vinegar and bring steadily to the boil or plunge them into boiling water, adding the salt and vinegar.
2. Cook for approximately 10 minutes.
3. When cooked and cool enough to handle they can be split and the intestinal vein removed as with lobster.
4. Shred the lettuce and add to the dill, together with a few nasturtium leaves, which may be shredded finely or left whole.
5. Blend all the ingredients together for the sauce and either serve this separately or blend the lettuce mixture with it.

Note: Crayfish are freshwater shellfish, similar to lobster in taste, but considerably smaller. Crawfish are like lobster but without the large claws.

Fish and vegetable platter

Cooking time: 30 minutes
Preparation time: 25 minutes
Main cooking utensils: saucepan, frying pan
Serves: 4–5

Imperial	Metric
1–1½ lb. mixed vegetables or the equivalent in frozen vegetables (see note)	½–¾ kg. mixed vegetables or the equivalent in frozen vegetables (see note)
seasoning	seasoning
1 oz. butter	25 g. butter
4–5 portions white fish (cod, turbot or halibut)	4–5 portions white fish (cod, turbot or halibut)
1 level tablespoon flour	1 level tablespoon flour
3 tablespoons oil	3 tablespoons oil
grated rind and juice of 1 lemon	grated rind and juice of 1 lemon
1 good tablespoon capers	1 good tablespoon capers
3–4 gherkins	3–4 gherkins
3–4 anchovy fillets	3–4 anchovy fillets
1 tablespoon chopped parsley	1 tablespoon chopped parsley
Garnish:	*Garnish:*
2 lemons	2 lemons

1. Prepare the vegetables and cook in boiling, salted water until just tender, drain and toss in butter.

2. Wash and dry the fish, coat in the flour, which should be seasoned well; do not exceed the small amount of flour since the fish should not have a thick coating.

3. Heat the oil and fry the fish in this until nearly tender on both sides.

4. Add the grated lemon rind, lemon juice, capers, diced gherkins and chopped anchovy fillets, heat thoroughly with the fish.

5. Lift the fish with the other ingredients from the pan, drain away any surplus oil.

6. Arrange the vegetables and fish with the capers, gherkins and anchovies on a hot dish, top with the chopped parsley and garnish with the lemons.

Note: A good mixture of flavour, colour and texture is given if beans and carrots are included in the vegetable selection.

Variation
Omit the anchovies and fry very finely chopped onion in the oil with the capers and gherkins.

Sole in cream sauce

Cooking time: 25–30 minutes
Preparation time: 15 minutes (classic version would take longer due to the garnishes)
Main cooking utensils: ovenproof dish, saucepan
Oven temperature: moderate (375°F., 190°C., Gas Mark 5)
Oven position: just above centre
Serves: 4

Imperial	Metric
seasoning	seasoning
4 large or 8 smaller fillets sole	4 large or 8 smaller fillets sole
1½ oz. butter	40 g. butter
2 shallots or small onions	2 shallots or small onions
good sprig parsley	good sprig parsley
1 small bay leaf	1 small bay leaf
12 tablespoons white wine	12 tablespoons white wine
Sauce:	*Sauce:*
1½ oz. butter	40 g. butter
1½ oz. flour	40 g. flour
½ pint thin cream	250 ml. thin cream
2 egg yolks	2 egg yolks
3 tablespoons thick cream	3 tablespoons thick cream
1 tablespoon lemon juice	1 tablespoon lemon juice
Garnish:	*Garnish:*
about 4 oz. cooked prunes	about 100 g. cooked prunes

1. Season the fillets of fish lightly and put into a buttered dish.
2. The fillets may either be folded or rolled, if the latter they take a little extra time to cook.
3. Add the chopped shallots or onions together with the herbs, do not chop the parsley.
4. Pour over the wine, cover the dish with well-buttered paper and cook until the fish is tender.
5. Melt the butter in the pan, stir in the flour, then add the cream to the roux. Stir in the strained liquid from the fish, bring the sauce to the boil, cook until thickened.
6. Whisk the egg yolks with the thick cream, add to the sauce with the lemon juice, and cook until thickened without boiling; season well.
7. In this version add the cooked prunes to the sauce, pour over the fish.

Note: The classic version of this dish is garnished with cooked mushrooms, mussels (using some of their liquid in the sauce), prawns, croûtons of fried bread or shapes of baked puff pastry.

Stuffed fillets of fish

Cooking time: 25–35 minutes
Preparation time: 20 minutes
Main cooking utensils: ovenproof baking dish, saucepan
Oven temperature: moderate (375°F., 190°C., Gas Mark 5)
Oven position: just above centre
Serves: 4

Imperial	Metric
4 large or 8 small fillets white fish	4 large or 8 small fillets white fish
2 oz. butter	50 g. butter
3 tablespoons fish stock or white wine	3 tablespoons fish stock or white wine
seasoning	seasoning
Stuffing:	*Stuffing:*
8 oz. firm-fleshed fish	200 g. firm-fleshed fish
2 oz. very fine soft breadcrumbs	50 g. very fine soft breadcrumbs
grated rind and juice of 1 lemon (or use a lime for change of flavour)	grated rind and juice of 1 lemon (or use a lime for change of flavour)
1 tablespoon olive oil or melted butter	1 tablespoon olive oil or melted butter
1 tablespoon finely chopped fresh herbs (see note)	1 tablespoon finely chopped fresh herbs (see note)
seasoning	seasoning
Garnish:	*Garnish:*
1 lb. green, French or runner beans	½ kg. green, French or runner beans
chopped herbs	chopped herbs
black olives	black olives

1. Cut the fish for stuffing into thin strips, blend with the other stuffing ingredients.
2. Roll the fillets loosely and put into a well-buttered baking dish.
3. Fill the rolls with the stuffing, piling this well above the fillets.
4. Pour the stock or wine into the dish, top each fillet with a piece of butter and season.
5. Cover the dish and bake until the fish is tender. The time depends on the size of the fillets but be sure that the stuffing as well as the fish is cooked.
6. While the fish is baking, cook the chopped or sliced beans. Arrange the fish on a hot dish with the beans, top with herbs and olives.

Note: Use marjoram, chervil, fennel, parsley.

Variation
Use sliced squid or shellfish in the stuffing.

Fish with fennel

Cooking time: 45–50 minutes
Preparation time: 25 minutes
Main cooking utensils: saucepan, ovenproof dish
Oven temperature: moderate (375°F., 190°C., Gas Mark 5)
Oven position: centre
Serves: 4–5

Imperial	Metric
about 12 small onions or shallots	about 12 small onions or shallots
3 oz. butter	75 g. butter
1 tablespoon oil	1 tablespoon oil
1 oz. flour	25 g. flour
1 tablespoon concentrated tomato purée or pulp of 2 large tomatoes	1 tablespoon concentrated tomato purée or pulp of 2 large tomatoes
$\frac{1}{2}$ pint cider or white wine	250 ml. cider or white wine
seasoning	seasoning
$\frac{1}{4}$ pint milk or thin cream	125 ml. milk or thin cream
1–2 teaspoons chopped fresh fennel leaves or $\frac{1}{2}$–1 teaspoon dried fennel	1–2 teaspoons chopped fresh fennel leaves or $\frac{1}{2}$–1 teaspoon dried fennel
$\frac{1}{2}$ teaspoon grated lemon rind	$\frac{1}{2}$ teaspoon grated lemon rind
whole fish weighing about 2$\frac{1}{2}$ lb. (sea bass, cod, fresh haddock or carp)	whole fish weighing about 1$\frac{1}{4}$ kg. (sea bass, cod, fresh haddock or carp)
several stalks fresh or dried fennel	several stalks fresh or dried fennel
about 12 tiny firm tomatoes	about 12 tiny firm tomatoes
Garnish:	*Garnish:*
parsley	parsley

1. Peel the onions or shallots, then toss in 2 oz. (50 g.) butter and the oil in the pan for several minutes.
2. Stir in the flour and cook for 2–3 minutes then blend in the tomato purée and cider or wine and cook until thickened slightly and smooth.
3. Season well, add the milk or cream but do not allow the sauce to boil. Add some fennel leaves or dried fennel and lemon rind.
4. Put the sauce into an ovenproof dish, top with the fish, brushed with the rest of the butter, add the fennel stalks and cover with foil or greaseproof paper.
5. Cook for approximately 30 minutes, then add the small tomatoes to the sauce and remove the foil so that the skin of the fish may brown slightly. Garnish with parsley.

Variation
Use red instead of white wine; add a crushed clove of garlic.

Halibut and orange

Cooking time: 15 minutes
Preparation time: 15 minutes plus time to marinate
Main cooking utensils: large saucepan, frying pan
Serves: 4

Imperial	Metric
4 portions of halibut (other white fish may be used, particularly turbot, brill, sole)	4 portions of halibut (other white fish may be used, particularly turbot, brill, sole)
juice of 2 oranges	juice of 2 oranges
2 tablespoons olive oil	2 tablespoons olive oil
seasoning	seasoning
1 clove garlic	1 clove garlic
Rice:	*Rice:*
4 oz. long-grain rice	100 g. long-grain rice
grated rind of 1 orange	grated rind of 1 orange
seasoning	seasoning
2 pints water	generous litre water
Garnish:	*Garnish:*
1–2 oranges	1–2 oranges
parsley	parsley

1. Wash and dry the fish well.

2. Blend the orange juice, oil, seasoning and crushed garlic, and pour this marinade into a fairly shallow dish.

3. Put the fish in this and leave for about 15 minutes, or a little longer if wished.

4. While the fish is standing, cook the rice by putting it with the orange rind and seasoning into 2 pints (generous litre) boiling water and cooking until just tender. Strain well, rinse in a sieve under cold water, spread out on a flat dish to dry in a very cool oven.

5. Pour any marinade left on the dish into the frying pan and cook the fish in this steadily until tender.

6. Slice the oranges and arrange them on the cooked rice on a hot serving dish. Top with the fish and sprinkle with parsley. Serve hot; no sauce is necessary as the fish is moist and full of flavour.

Variation

Add chopped herbs and chopped onion to the marinade and cook with the fish. Grill instead of frying the fish, baste with any marinade left.

Celebration dinner menu

Serves: 6–8

Turkey and cranberry soup

Melt 3 oz. (75 g.) butter, and fry 2 chopped onions, 2 chopped carrots and 2 chopped celery stalks until tender. Stir in $1\frac{1}{2}$ oz. (40 g.) flour, cook for 3 minutes. Blend in 2 pints (1 litre) turkey stock, 2 tablespoons finely chopped parsley and 4 tablespoons cranberry jelly. Cover the pan, simmer for 35 minutes, season well and top with chopped parsley.

Pork with lemon and apple stuffing

Score the skin on the leg of pork, brush with oil and season very lightly. Weigh the joint and allow 25 minutes cooking time per lb. ($\frac{1}{2}$ kg.) plus 25 minutes over. Start in a hot oven (425°F., 220°C., Gas Mark 7) and reduce the heat to moderately hot (400°F., 200°C., Gas Mark 6) after 40 minutes. Cut the tops off 6–8 small dessert apples, scoop out the centres, discard the cores and chop the flesh with 5 oz. (125 g.) breadcrumbs, grated rind and juice of 1 lemon, 1 large onion, finely chopped, 2 oz. (50 g.) melted butter and seasoning. Cook for about 30 minutes. Serve the pork on a hot dish surrounded by the stuffing.

Chocolate pear tipsy cake

Sieve together 6 oz. (150 g.) self-raising flour (or plain flour and $1\frac{1}{2}$ teaspoons baking powder) and 2 tablespoons cocoa, add 5 oz. (125 g.) soft brown sugar, 5 tablespoons corn oil, 5 tablespoons milk, 2 egg yolks and 1 teaspoon rum. Lastly fold in 2 stiffly whisked egg whites. Pour into a lined and greased 7-inch (18-cm.) cake tin and bake in the centre of a moderate oven (325–350°F., 170–180°C., Gas Mark 3–4) for about 50 minutes until firm to the touch. Turn out and cool then split and sandwich with whipped cream and sliced dessert pears (dipped in a little lemon juice). Top with whipped cream and curls of chocolate.

Apple and mincemeat sundaes

Cook $2\frac{1}{2}$ lb. ($1\frac{1}{4}$ kg.) peeled sliced apples with a very little water, lemon juice and sugar to taste. Beat to a smooth purée and tint a pale green. When cold fold in 3 stiffly whisked egg whites. Spoon layers of apple and mincemeat into sundae glasses. Top with whipped cream and glacé cherries.

Dutch celebration meal dishes

Serves: 4

Cheese and chicory hors d'oeuvre

Wash 2 heads of chicory and pull away 8 of the outer leaves. Chop the remainder of the leaves and put them into a bowl with 1 small onion (cut into rings), 1—2 tomatoes (cut into wedges) and 2 oz. (50 g.) diced Edam cheese. Blend with salad dressing, pile into individual bowls and garnish with the chicory leaves.

Pork and cheese crumble

Remove the bones and excess fat from 4 pork chops. Heat 1 oz. (25 g.) butter in a frying pan, fry the chops in this until golden brown. Peel and slice 2 medium-sized onions thinly; put them into an ovenproof dish and cover with a large can of tomatoes. Season and add 1 teaspoon sugar. Place the chops on top of the tomatoes. Blend 5 oz. (125 g.) soft white breadcrumbs with 4 oz. (100 g.) grated Gouda cheese. Sprinkle over the chops and bake for 1 hour in the centre of a moderate oven (325°F., 170°C., Gas Mark 3). Lift the lid and continue cooking for another 30 minutes. Serve topped with raw or fried onion rings.

Lemon chiffon flan

Cream 3 oz. (75 g.) butter with 1 level tablespoon golden syrup. Crush 6 oz. (150 g.) digestive biscuits, and work these into the butter mixture with 1 teaspoon ground cinnamon. Line an 8-inch (20-cm.) flan dish or flan ring on a serving plate with this. Put it into the refrigerator for several hours to chill. Meanwhile dissolve a lemon-flavoured jelly in $\frac{1}{2}$ pint (275 ml.) water, add the grated rind and juice of 1 lemon, cool and stiffen slightly. Whisk hard with a small can evaporated milk. Spoon into the flan case and when firm decorate with whipped cream and crystallised lemon slices.

American Thanksgiving menu

Serves: 6–8

Prawn and citrus fruit cocktail
Remove the pulp from 2 large oranges and 1 grapefruit. Blend with a 5-oz. (142-ml.) carton dairy soured cream or whipped thick cream plus the juice of $\frac{1}{2}$–1 lemon. Add 2 tablespoons mayonnaise, 1 teaspoon tomato ketchup and 4–6 oz. (100–150 g.) shelled prawns. Put into glasses, top with prawns and a little tomato ketchup.

Roast turkey with celery and herb stuffing
Mix 8 oz. (200 g.) soft crumbs from a brown or wholemeal loaf with 8 stalks finely chopped celery, 3 tablespoons chopped parsley, 1 teaspoon chopped lemon thyme, the grated rind and juice of 1 lemon, 1 finely chopped onion, 4 oz. (100 g.) shredded suet or melted margarine and 2 eggs or 3 egg yolks. Put into an 8- to 10-lb. (4- to $4\frac{3}{4}$-kg.) turkey; either cook in a very moderate oven allowing 30 minutes per lb. ($\frac{1}{2}$ kg.) and 30 minutes over or in a hot oven allowing 15 minutes per lb. ($\frac{1}{2}$ kg.) and 15 minutes over. Baste well with melted fat or butter. Always allow frozen turkeys to defrost before cooking. Serve with roast potatoes, corn and beans and cranberry and apple sauce.

Cranberry and apple sauce
Simmer 1 lb. ($\frac{1}{2}$ kg.) peeled apples and 8 oz. (200 g.) cranberries with $\frac{1}{4}$ pint (150 ml.) water and 3–4 oz. (75–100 g.) sugar until tender.

Coffee chiffon
Make 1 pint (500 ml.) strong coffee. Soften $\frac{3}{4}$ oz. (20 g.) gelatine in a little cold coffee, stir into the hot coffee and heat until dissolved. Allow to cool and stiffen slightly then fold in $\frac{1}{2}$ pint (250 ml.) lightly whipped cream, 2–3 oz. (50–75 g.) finely chopped pecans or walnuts. Whisk 3 egg whites (left from the stuffing) very stiffly, gradually whisk in 2–3 oz. (50–75 g.) castor sugar and fold into the coffee nut mixture. Pile into a dish, serve with sweet biscuits.

Skewer-cooked spiced chicken livers

Cooking time: 20 minutes
Preparation time: 15 minutes
Main cooking utensils: saucepan, 4 skewers (to fit frying pan),
   large frying pan
Serves: 4

Imperial	Metric
6 oz. long-grain rice	150 g. long-grain rice
$\frac{3}{5}$ pint water	300 ml. water
seasoning	seasoning
grated rind and juice of 1 lemon	grated rind and juice of 1 lemon
1–2 teaspoons curry seasoning or curry powder	1–2 teaspoons curry seasoning or curry powder
1 lb. chicken livers	$\frac{1}{2}$ kg. chicken livers
8 oz. mushrooms	200 g. mushrooms
4 oz. butter	100 g. butter
little chopped parsley	little chopped parsley
$\frac{1}{4}$ pint Madeira	125 ml. Madeira
Garnish:	*Garnish:*
tomato	tomato
parsley	parsley

1. Put the rice into a saucepan with the cold water, seasoning, grated rind and juice of $\frac{1}{2}$ lemon and curry seasoning or powder.
2. Bring to the boil, stir, cover the pan and simmer for 15 minutes.
3. Put the chicken livers on to skewers with a few of the mushrooms; season.
4. Fry in the hot butter, turning once or twice in the pan, and cook for 8–10 minutes. Lift out and keep warm.
5. Add the remaining mushrooms, sliced or whole, to the pan with a little chopped parsley, the remaining grated lemon rind and juice and the Madeira.
6. Simmer until the mushrooms are tender, about 5 minutes.
7. Put the rice on a hot dish with the skewered meat and the sauce. Garnish with tomato and parsley.

Note: Canned mushrooms could be used in this dish. As they are often canned in brine, season very lightly and use less lemon.

Variation
Use calf's or lamb's liver, or diced fillet or rump steak instead of the chicken livers.

Tongue with almond sauce

Cooking time: 1½ hours
Preparation time: 30 minutes
Main cooking utensil: saucepan
Serves: 6

Imperial	Metric
6–8 small calves' or lambs' tongues	6–8 small calves' or lambs' tongues
water	water
seasoning	seasoning
bay leaf	bay leaf
2 onions	2 onions
4–6 carrots	4–6 carrots
Sauce:	*Sauce:*
4 oz. fat pork or bacon	100 g. fat pork or bacon
1 oz. butter	25 g. butter
1 oz. flour	25 g. flour
just over $\frac{1}{2}$ pint stock	275 ml. stock
2 oz. ground almonds or finely chopped almonds	50 g. ground almonds or finely chopped almonds
grated rind and juice of 1 lemon	grated rind and juice of 1 lemon
2 oz. raisins (optional)	50 g. raisins (optional)
$\frac{1}{4}$ pint red wine	125 ml. red wine
Garnish:	*Garnish:*
chopped parsley	chopped parsley
cooked peas	cooked peas

1. Put the whole tongues with water to cover, seasoning and the bay leaf into a pan, add the finely chopped onions.

2. Simmer for 45 minutes, then add the sliced carrots, cook for a further 30 minutes.

3. Allow to cool sufficiently to handle. Skin and halve the tongues.

4. Dice the pork and fry it in a pan with the butter, stir in the flour, gradually blend in the generous $\frac{1}{2}$ pint (275 ml.) strained stock.

5. Bring to the boil and cook until thickened, add the almonds, lemon rind and juice, raisins and wine. Blend well, add the sliced carrots and tongues. Do not add the onions.

6. Put half the tongues into a hot dish, top with the sauce. Arrange the rest of the tongues on top with the parsley and peas.

Lamb with mushroom sauce

Cooking time: 1 hour 10 minutes
Preparation time: 15 minutes
Main cooking utensils: roasting tin, saucepan
Oven temperature: hot (425–450°F., 220–230°C., Gas Mark 7–8)
   then moderately hot (375–400°F., 190–200°C., Gas Mark 5–6)
Oven position: above centre
Serves: 4

Imperial	Metric
2½ lb. loin of lamb	1¼ kg. loin of lamb
3 oz. butter	75 g. butter
seasoning	seasoning
8 oz. small mushrooms	200 g. small mushrooms
1 oz. flour	25 g. flour
½ pint white stock	250 ml. white stock
2 tablespoons brandy (optional)	2 tablespoons brandy (optional)
2 tablespoons thin cream	2 tablespoons thin cream
1 tablespoon chopped marjoram or oregano (wild marjoram)	1 tablespoon chopped marjoram or oregano (wild marjoram)
4 large or 8 smaller tomatoes	4 large or 8 smaller tomatoes

1. Brush the lean part of the lamb with some of the butter.

2. Roast until tender, allowing 20 minutes per lb. (½ kg.) and 20 minutes over, and reducing the heat from hot to moderately hot after about 30 minutes.

3. Towards the end of the cooking time, spoon a little lamb dripping into a saucepan, add the remaining butter and toss the well-seasoned mushrooms in this. Lift out, keep hot, blend in the flour, cook for several minutes, then gradually blend in the stock.

4. Bring to the boil, cook until thickened, add the brandy, if used, and cream, replace the mushrooms and add half the marjoram or oregano.

5. Bake the tomatoes until just soft, seasoning them well.

6. Put the mushrooms and sauce round the meat, add the tomatoes and top with the remaining marjoram or oregano.

Garlic-flavoured lamb

Cooking time: 20 minutes per lb. ($\frac{1}{2}$ kg.) and 20 minutes over
Preparation time: 15 minutes
Main cooking utensil: roasting tin
Oven temperature: hot (425°F., 220°C., Gas Mark 7) then moderately
   hot (400°F., 200°C., Gas Mark 6)
Serves: 6

Imperial	Metric
1–2 cloves garlic	1–2 cloves garlic
1 small leg or shoulder of young lamb	1 small leg or shoulder of young lamb
4 oz. butter	100 g. butter
French mustard	French mustard
pepper	pepper
little flour	little flour

1. Peel the garlic cloves and slice them thinly lengthwise into slivers. Make slits in the meat and push the garlic slivers into the cuts.

2. Spread the meat with the butter and a thin layer of mustard.

3. Sprinkle lightly with pepper and a little flour to give a crisp finish to the meat.

4. Roast in a hot oven, reducing the heat to moderately hot after the first 20 minutes. Serve the lamb with matchstick potatoes, made by frying tiny strips of potato until golden brown and crisp.

Note: This method of cooking lamb with garlic is suitable for very young lamb, which is not too fat. Older meat is more fatty and with the generous amount of butter in the recipe would give a greasy result.

Variation

Very young lamb is usually served underdone in France, where this recipe comes from. Roast the meat for 15 minutes per lb. ($\frac{1}{2}$ kg.) and 15 minutes over if you prefer lamb less well cooked.

Lamb cutlets with prunes

Cooking time: $\frac{3}{4}$–$1\frac{1}{4}$ hours (see stage 1)
Preparation time: 10 minutes plus overnight soaking of prunes
Main cooking utensils: saucepan, large frying pan
Serves: 4

Imperial	Metric
8 oz. dried prunes (see stage 1)	200 g. dried prunes (see stage 1)
2 tablespoons apricot preserve or jam	2 tablespoons apricot preserve or jam
grated rind of 1 lemon	grated rind of 1 lemon
$\frac{1}{2}$ tablespoon lemon juice or vinegar	$\frac{1}{2}$ tablespoon lemon juice or vinegar
little sugar (optional)	little sugar (optional)
2 oz. fat	50 g. fat
about 8 tiny onions	about 8 tiny onions
seasoning	seasoning
1 level tablespoon flour or potato flour	1 level tablespoon flour or potato flour
good pinch paprika	good pinch paprika
good pinch dried mixed herbs or few fresh mixed herbs	good pinch dried mixed herbs or few fresh mixed herbs
8 small lamb chops	8 small lamb chops
Garnish:	*Garnish:*
chopped parsley	chopped parsley

1. Soak the prunes overnight with enough water to cover. Simmer gently for about 1 hour until just tender, do not make them too soft; if using the 'tenderised' prunes, pour over boiling water and simmer for about 30 minutes without soaking.
2. Lift the prunes out of the liquid. If necessary boil the liquid until about 12 tablespoons remain, stir in the apricot preserve and grated lemon rind and juice. The liquid should have a semi-sweet taste. If a sweeter flavour is required add a little sugar to the prunes whilst cooking.
3. Heat the fat in a pan, fry the onions until golden brown.
4. Blend the seasoning, flour, paprika and herbs, dust the chops with this, add to the pan with the onions. Cook steadily until crisp and golden brown.
5. Add the prunes and the prune liquid 3–4 minutes before the end of the cooking time. Top with chopped parsley. This is excellent with green beans.

Note: If you have only a small pan cook the onions first and keep warm then cook the meat.

Cutlets in white wine sauce

Cooking time: 25 minutes
Preparation time: 15 minutes
Main cooking utensils: 2 frying pans
Serves: 4

Imperial	Metric
4 chops or cutlets of lamb or young mutton	4 chops or cutlets of lamb or young mutton
seasoning	seasoning
1–2 large onions	1–2 large onions
1–2 cloves garlic	1–2 cloves garlic
2 tablespoons oil	2 tablespoons oil
1 lb. boiled potatoes	$\frac{1}{2}$ kg. boiled potatoes
3 oz. margarine or butter	75 g. margarine or butter
1 oz. flour	25 g. flour
$\frac{1}{4}$ pint white wine and $\frac{1}{2}$ pint white stock or $\frac{1}{2}$ pint wine and $\frac{1}{4}$ pint stock	125 ml. white wine and 250 ml. white stock or 250 ml. wine and 125 ml. stock
8 medium-sized pickled gherkins or 3-inch piece cucumber and 2 teaspoons vinegar	8 medium-sized pickled gherkins or 3-inch piece cucumber and 2 teaspoons vinegar
Garnish:	*Garnish:*
chopped parsley	chopped parsley

1. Trim any excess fat from the chops (the butcher will have prepared cutlets) and season well.
2. Peel and slice the onions, crush the garlic.
3. Fry the meat with the onions and garlic in the oil so that the flavours blend together.
4. When the meat is tender, keep hot on a dish, but leave the onions and garlic in the pan.
5. Meanwhile slice the potatoes, heat gently in the butter in a second pan.
6. Blend the flour with the wine and stock, add to the onions and bring to the boil, cook until thickened. Add the sliced or diced, drained gherkins or cucumber and vinegar and simmer for 5 minutes.
7. Put the meat and potatoes on to a dish, top with the sauce, and garnish with the parsley. This is excellent with salad and more pickled gherkins or other vinegar pickle.

Variation
Add sliced olives instead of gherkins or cucumber.

Lamb cutlets in pastry cases

Cooking time: 45–50 minutes
Preparation time: 15 minutes
Main cooking utensils: frying or grill pan, baking tray
Oven temperature: moderately hot to hot (400–425°F., 200–220°C., Gas Mark 6–7) then very moderate (325–350°F., 170–180°C., Gas Mark 3–4)
Oven position: just above centre
Serves: 6

Imperial	Metric
6 large lamb cutlets	6 large lamb cutlets
seasoning	seasoning
$\frac{1}{2}$ tablespoon chopped chives	$\frac{1}{2}$ tablespoon chopped chives
1 teaspoon chopped mint	1 teaspoon chopped mint
Pastry:	*Pastry:*
10–12 oz. plain flour	250–300 g. plain flour
pinch salt	pinch salt
6 oz. butter	150 g. butter
water to bind	water to bind
Glaze:	*Glaze:*
1 egg	1 egg

1. Grill or fry the lamb cutlets for about 5–10 minutes depending upon thickness, season, sprinkle with chopped chives and mint. Allow to cool.

2. Meanwhile, make the pastry. Sieve the flour and salt, rub in the butter, bind with water to form a rolling consistency.

3. Roll out thinly and cut into triangles large enough to cover meat.

4. Lay a cutlet on each triangle of pastry. Brush the edges with water, wrap round the meat. Garnish with leaves of pastry and brush with beaten egg.

5. Bake for approximately 25 minutes in a moderately hot to hot oven, then lower the heat to very moderate and leave for a further 15 minutes.

6. Serve hot with flageolets or young broad beans tossed in butter and chopped parsley.

Variation
Spread the cutlets with a stuffing made of pork sausage meat and chopped herbs, then wrap in pastry.

Lamb with peppercorns

Cooking time: 45 minutes
Preparation time: 20 minutes
Main cooking utensils: 2 saucepans, grill pan, ovenproof serving dish
Oven temperature: very moderate (350°F., 180°C., Gas Mark 4)
Oven position: centre
Serves: 6

Imperial	Metric
6 large lamb chops	6 large lamb chops
6 oz. butter	150 g. butter
about 24–30 peppercorns (depending on taste)	about 24–30 peppercorns (depending on taste)
Duchesse potatoes:	*Duchesse potatoes:*
2¼ lb. potatoes (weight when peeled)	generous 1 kg. potatoes (weight when peeled)
3 oz. butter	75 g. butter
3 egg yolks	3 egg yolks
seasoning	seasoning
Garnish:	*Garnish:*
3 large tomatoes	3 large tomatoes
1½ lb. French beans	¾ kg. French beans
parsley	parsley

1. Cut away the bone from each chop so that the meat may be rolled into a round called a noisette.
2. Brush the lean part of the meat with a little melted butter, press the crushed peppercorns into one side of the meat, turn the noisettes over and repeat on the second side.
3. Boil the potatoes in salted water until just soft, strain and mash, add the butter, egg yolks and seasoning. Divide into 12 portions and form into 12 cakes with a palette knife.
4. Heat half the butter in a pan, fry rounds of Duchesse potatoes until golden coloured on both sides.
5. Put on a hot dish, top half the rounds with halved, seasoned tomatoes; heat these in the oven while frying the noisettes.
6. Fry the noisettes in the remaining butter until tender.
7. Lift the noisettes on to the rounds of Duchesse potatoes, put on to a serving dish with the drained cooked beans and parsley.

Variation
Omit the peppercorns and press freshly chopped herbs into the lamb.

Loin of pork with prunes

Cooking time: 15 minutes plus time for cooking and soaking prunes
Preparation time: few minutes
Main cooking utensils: saucepan, frying pan
Serves: 4

Imperial	Metric
4–6 oz. prunes	100–150 g. prunes
little sugar	little sugar
1–1½ lb. loin or fillet of pork	½–¾ kg. loin or fillet of pork
seasoning	seasoning
3–4 oz. butter	75–100 g. butter
glass schnapps or brandy	glass schnapps or brandy

1. Soak the prunes for several hours, or overnight, in water to cover, then simmer until tender with sugar to taste.

2. Cut the pork into neat pieces.

3. Season lightly, then fry in butter until tender, adding the prunes towards the end of the cooking time.

4. Add the schnapps or brandy, heat gently, then ignite and serve. Serve with boiled potatoes, topped with chopped dill, and cooked peas or beans.

To ignite brandy and other spirits: Make sure that you have a sufficient quantity, this is important when adding brandy to a very liquid mixture, and that it is warm before trying to light it.

Variation

Flavour pork with a little powdered ginger; fry a finely chopped onion in a pan with the pork; use sliced apples instead of prunes; add a little thin cream to the butter at stage 3.

Loin of pork with piquant sauce

Cooking time: approximately 3 hours
Preparation time: 10 minutes
Main cooking utensils: deep covered casserole, saucepan
Oven temperature: moderate (350–375°F., 180–190°C., Gas Mark 4–5)
Oven position: centre
Serves: 8–10

Imperial	Metric
1 loin of pork, approximately 5 lb. in weight	1 loin of pork, approximately 2½ kg. in weight
Glaze:	*Glaze:*
8-oz. can pineapple pieces	226-g. can pineapple pieces
½ pint water	300 ml. water
2 oz. black treacle	50 g. black treacle
1 level teaspoon dry mustard	1 level teaspoon dry mustard
1 level teaspoon salt	1 level teaspoon salt
¼ level teaspoon pepper	¼ level teaspoon pepper
½ oz. cornflour	15 g. cornflour
1 stock cube	1 stock cube
1 tablespoon redcurrant jelly	1 tablespoon redcurrant jelly
1 tablespoon vinegar	1 tablespoon vinegar

1. Place the meat in a tin or casserole.
2. Drain the pineapple and mix the juice with the water.
3. Blend the treacle, mustard, salt and pepper with the fruit juice and water.
4. Pour this over the meat, cover with foil or a lid and cook, basting every 30 minutes.
5. Remove the cover 30 minutes before the end.
6. When cooked, transfer the meat to a heated dish.
7. Blend the cornflour, crushed stock cube, redcurrant jelly, vinegar and the liquid from the baking tin, bring to the boil on top of the cooker, stirring all the time.
8. Chop the pineapple and add this to the sauce, re-season. Serve with sprigged cauliflower or carrots tossed in melted butter.

Note: This is delicious served cold with salad.

Variation
Use golden syrup instead of treacle.

Sweet and sour pork

Cooking time: 30 minutes
Preparation time: 30 minutes
Preparation time: 20 minutes
Main cooking utensils: saucepan, frying pan
Serves: 3–4

Imperial	Metric
1 lb. fairly lean pork (a slice from the leg is ideal)	$\frac{1}{2}$ kg. fairly lean pork (a slice from the leg is ideal)
1 oz. cornflour	25 g. cornflour
seasoning	seasoning
good pinch monosodium glutamate	good pinch monosodium glutamate
good pinch powdered ginger	good pinch powdered ginger
Sweet and sour sauce:	*Sweet and sour sauce:*
2 oz. spring onions	50 g. spring onions
1 tablespoon oil	1 tablespoon oil
1 tablespoon cornflour	1 tablespoon cornflour
2 tablespoons vinegar	2 tablespoons vinegar
1–2 tablespoons tomato purée	1–2 tablespoons tomato purée
$\frac{1}{2}$–1 tablespoon soy sauce	$\frac{1}{2}$–1 tablespoon soy sauce
$\frac{1}{2}$ pint water	250 ml. water
1 oz. brown sugar	25 g. brown sugar

1. First make the sauce. Dice the spring onions very finely and toss in hot oil until just tender.
2. Blend the cornflour with the vinegar, tomato purée, soy sauce, water and sugar and add to the onions. Simmer until thickened.
3. Meanwhile, dice the pork. Mix the cornflour with the seasonings and coat the pork in the seasoned cornflour.
4. When the sauce is thickened, fry the pork in hot oil until crisp and golden brown.
5. Serve the pork topped with the sauce, with plain boiled rice.

Variation
Sweet and sour pork and chicken: Joint a 2- to 2$\frac{1}{2}$-lb. (1-kg.) chicken and fry in oil, or dice the meat and coat with seasoned flour, then fry with the pork. Pour the sauce over the meats and serve garnished with tomatoes and parsley. This serves 6–8.

Apricot-glazed gammon

Cooking time: 2 hours
Preparation time: 15 minutes
Main cooking utensil: ovenproof dish
Oven temperature: moderate (375°F., 190°C., Gas Mark 5)
Oven position: centre
Serves: 8

Imperial	Metric
4 lb. gammon (see note)	2 kg. gammon (see note)
2 bay leaves	2 bay leaves
1 medium can apricot halves	1 medium can apricot halves
Garnish:	*Garnish:*
watercress	watercress
glacé cherries	glacé cherries

1. Soak gammon for several hours in cold water if a milder flavour is preferred. Then place in an ovenproof dish with the bay leaves.
2. Pour over enough boiling water to half cover the gammon.
3. Cover the dish with aluminium foil and bake for $1\frac{1}{4}$ hours.
4. Remove from the oven and strain off the bacon stock.
5. Remove the skin from the meat and stand the gammon in the ovenproof dish.
6. Strain the juice from the apricots over the gammon and return to the oven for a further 45 minutes, basting frequently with the syrup.
7. Remove the gammon from the oven and score a diagonal design on the fat with a sharp knife. Garnish with apricot halves, watercress and halved cherries. Serve hot or cold with salad.

Note: For a more economical joint use forehock or collar, but these may need longer cooking. Use the bacon stock for soup; lentil soup is particularly good with this.

Variation
Use pineapple rings instead of apricots.

Rolled stuffed veal

Cooking time: 2 hours 20 minutes
Preparation time: 20 minutes
Main cooking utensils: frying pan, roasting tin
Oven temperature: moderately hot to hot (400–425°F., 200–220°C.,
    Gas Mark 6–7)
Oven position: hottest part
Serves: 6–7

Imperial	Metric
1 3-lb. boned joint veal (loin, shoulder or leg)	1 1½-kg. boned joint veal (loin, shoulder or leg)
2–3 oz. fat for basting	50–75 g. fat for basting
Stuffing:	*Stuffing:*
2 oz. butter	50 g. butter
4–5 large tomatoes	4–5 large tomatoes
1 green pepper	1 green pepper
1 red pepper	1 red pepper
2 onions	2 onions
6 oz. fat pork or bacon	150 g. fat pork or bacon
seasoning	seasoning
1 teaspoon mixed chopped fresh herbs or good pinch dried herbs	1 teaspoon mixed chopped fresh herbs or good pinch dried herbs

1. Cut the boned veal to make 2 'pockets', leave the very bottom of the meat uncut.

2. To make the stuffing, heat the butter, and fry the skinned, sliced tomatoes, strips of green and red pepper (discard the seeds and core) and finely chopped onions.

3. Blend with the strips of fat pork or bacon, seasoning and chopped herbs.

4. Insert a quarter of the mixture into the first pocket, another quarter into the second and spread half the rest over the top of the veal.

5. Roll, tie or skewer. If possible put it under a board with a weight on top (for easy slicing).

6. Brown the veal in hot fat in a tin, then roast for 1 hour, basting several times with the hot fat.

7. Spread the remaining stuffing mixture on the top of the meat and continue cooking for another hour.

8. When the veal is cooked, remove the string or skewers and slice.

Variation
Other stuffings may be used.

Veal or beef with spring vegetables

Cooking time: see stage 3
Preparation time: 30 minutes
Main cooking utensils: roasting tin, saucepan
Oven temperature: hot (425–450°F., 220–230°C., Gas Mark 7–8) then
    moderately hot (400°F., 200°C., Gas Mark 6)
Oven position: above centre
Serves: 8

Imperial	Metric
12 oz. fat from bacon or fat pork	300 g. fat from bacon or fat pork
about 3½–4 lb. meat (see note)	about 1½–1¾ kg. meat (see note)
1 pint red wine	550 ml. red wine
1½ lb. small onions	¾ kg. small onions
8 oz. mushrooms	200 g. mushrooms
1½–2 lb. carrots	¾–1 kg. carrots
2 lb. peas	1 kg. peas

1. Cut the fat into long thin strips, put it into a larding needle (or use a carpet needle) and thread through the meat.
2. Cover the outside with more fat bacon.
3. For veal allow 25 minutes per lb. (½ kg.) and 25 minutes over, for beef allow 15–20 minutes to the lb. (½ kg.) and 15–20 minutes over. Roast in a hot oven, reducing the heat to moderately hot after 1½ hours if wished.
4. At the end of 1 hour pour the wine into the roasting tin, baste the meat and continue basting at 30 minute intervals.
5. Add the onions 45 minutes before the end of the cooking time, and add the mushrooms 15 minutes before the end of the cooking time.
6. Meanwhile cook the carrots in boiling, salted water for about 15 minutes.
7. Add the peas and continue cooking until both vegetables are tender.
8. Serve the veal hot with the vegetables. If wished the liquid may be thickened.

Note: Choose a joint of veal fillet or boned and rolled loin, beef topside or fresh brisket, châteaubriand steak or sirloin.

Variation
Other vegetables can be used, for example, young turnips, celeriac or young parsnips; cook these with the carrots.

Veal escalopes and mushrooms

Cooking time: 15–20 minutes
Preparation time: 10 minutes
Main cooking utensil: large frying pan
Serves: 4

Imperial	Metric
4 oz. butter	100 g. butter
4 slices fillet of veal (see note)	4 slices fillet of veal (see note)
seasoning	seasoning
sprig tarragon	sprig tarragon
8 oz. mushrooms (see note)	200 g. mushrooms (see note)
½ pint thin cream	275 ml. thin cream
Garnish:	*Garnish:*
small sprigs tarragon	small sprigs tarragon

1. Heat the butter, then fry the slices of well-seasoned veal steadily until golden brown.
2. Lift on to a dish and keep hot.
3. Chop the tarragon finely and mix with the sliced mushrooms, season well, then fry these steadily until soft.
4. Arrange the mushrooms on the dish with the meat.
5. Stir the cream into the pan and blend with the meat and vegetable juices.
6. Either pour the cream sauce over the meat or serve separately.
7. Garnish the escalopes with sprigs of tarragon.
8. Serve hot with vegetables or salad, or this is ideal to cook in a large pan over a barbecue. Use a large pan, fry the veal, push to one side of the pan while cooking the mushrooms, then add the cream.

Note: Veal fillet is cut from the top of the leg. If the slices are too thick, beat them out thinly with a mallet or rolling pin. Girolles are a type of edible fungi, not unlike mushrooms in flavour but of a firmer texture, ordinary mushrooms could be used instead.

Variation

Instead of slices of veal, thin slices of pork could be used, or thin fillet steaks. Tarragon is a herb that blends with all these meats as well as with fish.

Fried veal and cream sauce

Cooking time: 20 minutes
Preparation time: 20 minutes, plus time to infuse milk
Main cooking utensils: saucepan, frying pan, also frying pan and
    saucepan for vegetables
Serves: 5

Imperial	Metric
5 rounds bread	5 rounds bread
3 oz. butter	75 g. butter
5 rounds fillet of veal	5 rounds fillet of veal
Sauce:	*Sauce:*
just over $\frac{1}{2}$ pint milk	275 ml. milk
$\frac{1}{2}$ carrot	$\frac{1}{2}$ carrot
$\frac{1}{2}$ onion	$\frac{1}{2}$ onion
1 stalk celery	1 stalk celery
few peppercorns	few peppercorns
1 oz. butter	25 g. butter
1 oz. flour	25 g. flour
2 teaspoons capers	2 teaspoons capers
1 teaspoon chopped tarragon	1 teaspoon chopped tarragon
3 tablespoons thick cream	3 tablespoons thick cream
seasoning	seasoning

1. First make the sauce. Infuse the milk with the carrot, onion, celery and peppercorns by heating it and standing it in a warm place.

2. Strain the milk. Melt the butter in a pan, stir in the flour, cook for several minutes. Add the milk, bring to the boil and cook until thickened, stirring well. Add the capers, tarragon, cream and seasoning. Keep hot (see note).

3. Meanwhile fry the rounds of bread in hot butter, put them on to a hot serving dish, then fry the veal until tender.

4. Put the veal on to the fried bread, top with the sauce, serve with sauté potatoes and Julienne carrots and celeriac or turnip.

Note: This dish needs careful preparation and timing. Make the sauce and transfer it to a double saucepan, and cover with a damp paper to prevent a skin forming. Cook the veal, put it on to a hot dish, cover with foil so that it does not dry and keep it hot in the oven.

Fillets of veal with mushrooms

Cooking time: 25 minutes
Preparation time: 10 minutes
Main cooking utensils: 2 frying pans
Serves: 4

Imperial	Metric
8 small pieces fillet of veal, cut very thinly	8 small pieces fillet of veal, cut very thinly
seasoning	seasoning
4 oz. butter or 3 oz. butter and 1 tablespoon oil	100 g. butter or 75 g. butter and 1 tablespoon oil
1 oz. flour	25 g. flour
$\frac{1}{4}$ pint milk	125 ml. milk
$\frac{1}{4}$ pint white stock or water and chicken stock cube	125 ml. white stock or water and chicken stock cube
$\frac{1}{4}$ pint thin cream or half thick cream and half water	125 ml. thin cream or half thick cream and half water
2 tablespoons very dry sherry (optional)	2 tablespoons very dry sherry (optional)
4–6 oz. mushrooms	100–150 g. mushrooms
Garnish:	*Garnish:*
parsley	parsley

1. Roll the veal neatly and secure it with wooden cocktail sticks. Season lightly.
2. Fry in 3 oz. (75 g.) of the butter until tender, but keep the heat sufficiently low so that they do not brown.
3. Lift out of the pan, blend in the flour and cook for several minutes, then gradually work in the milk and stock.
4. Bring to the boil, stir until thickened, add the cream, seasoning, and the sherry, if wished.
5. Meanwhile fry the sliced mushrooms in the remaining butter, stir into the sauce and pour over the veal rolls. Garnish with parsley.

Note: By frying the mushrooms separately, then adding them to the sauce you keep this a better colour. If the dish is to be kept waiting, make the sauce a little thinner. Cover the whole dish with foil and keep it warm in a cool oven.

Tournedos of fillet steak with herbs

Cooking time: 15 minutes
Preparation time: 15 minutes
Main cooking utensils: saucepan for fat or oil and frying basket,
   frying pan
Serves: 4

Imperial	Metric
1 lb. potatoes (weight when peeled)	$\frac{1}{2}$ kg. potatoes (weight when peeled)
fat or oil for frying	fat or oil for frying
4 medium-sized fillet steaks	4 medium-sized fillet steaks
4 strips bacon fat	4 strips bacon fat
seasoning	seasoning
$\frac{1}{2}$–1 teaspoon mixed dried tarragon or rosemary	$\frac{1}{2}$–1 teaspoon mixed dried tarragon or rosemary
3 oz. butter	75 g. butter
Garnish:	*Garnish:*
parsley	parsley
tomatoes	tomatoes

1. Peel the potatoes, cut them into matchstick shapes, dry well.
2. Fry them steadily in hot fat or oil until tender and pale golden, but not brown. Lift out of the pan.
3. Form each steak into a round shape with your hands, arrange the bacon fat round the sides and tie with fine string.
4. Season lightly, press the herbs into both sides of the meat very firmly with the back of a knife.
5. Heat the butter and fry the steaks; allow 2 minutes over a fairly high heat on each side for very rare steaks, then lower the heat and cook for a further 4–6 minutes according to personal taste.
6. Meanwhile, re-heat the fat or oil, put in the matchstick potatoes, fry until crisp and drain on absorbent paper.
7. Arrange the potatoes on individual plates, top with a tournedos, garnish with parsley and segments of tomato, serve with salad.

Note: To save time, heat commercial potato crisps instead of making matchstick potatoes.

Tournedos à la Rossini

Cooking time: see stage 4
Preparation time: few minutes
Main cooking utensils: large frying pan, pan for potatoes
Serves: 4

Imperial	Metric
4 fillet steaks	4 fillet steaks
4 slices of bread	4 slices of bread
3 oz. butter or 2 oz. butter and 1 tablespoon oil	75 g. butter or 50 g. butter and 1 tablespoon oil
Sauce:	*Sauce:*
4 tablespoons brown stock	4 tablespoons brown stock
4 tablespoons Madeira	4 tablespoons Madeira
Garnish:	*Garnish:*
4 slices pâté	4 slices pâté
4 truffles (see note)	4 truffles (see note)

1. Tie the meat into rounds, unless this has been done by the butcher.

2. Fry rounds or squares of bread in hot butter or butter and oil until crisp and golden brown.

3. Put onto a hot dish and keep warm.

4. Fry the meat on both sides. For underdone steak this should be served almost at once without further cooking; for medium-done steak, cook for 2—3 minutes each side, lower the heat and cook for a further 2—3 minutes; for well done steak, cook on each side for 2—3 minutes, then allow a further 4—5 minutes. Lift on to the bread.

5. Blend the stock and Madeira together in the pan, and pour round the steaks.

6. Top with pâté and truffles. Serve at once with sauté potatoes and watercress.

Note: If you cannot get truffles use cooked mushrooms instead. You can grill the steaks instead of frying them if you prefer.

Sauté potatoes

Fry diced or sliced cooked potatoes in hot fat until brown.

Meatballs with cheese

Cooking time: 10–15 minutes
Preparation time: 20 minutes
Main cooking utensils: frying pan, skewers and grill pan
Serves: 4

Imperial	Metric
Meatballs:	*Meatballs:*
12 oz. beef (rump steak, sirloin or topside)	300 g. beef (rump steak, sirloin or topside)
4 oz. bacon	100 g. bacon
1 onion	1 onion
pinch oregano (wild marjoram)	pinch oregano (wild marjoram)
little grated nutmeg	little grated nutmeg
seasoning	seasoning
2 oz. breadcrumbs	50 g. breadcrumbs
little stock or milk (optional)	little stock or milk (optional)
To coat:	*To coat:*
1 oz. seasoned flour or 1 egg and 2 oz. crisp breadcrumbs	25 g. seasoned flour or 1 egg and 50 g. crisp breadcrumbs
To fry:	*To fry:*
2 oz. butter	50 g. butter
1 tablespoon oil	1 tablespoon oil
Cheese topping:	*Cheese topping:*
8 oz. Bel Paese, Mozzarella or Gruyère cheese	200 g. Bel Paese, Mozzarella or Gruyère cheese

1. Put the meat, bacon and onion through the mincer at least once.
2. Blend with the rest of the ingredients for the meatballs.
3. If dry, blend with a little stock or milk.
4. Form into balls, roll either in seasoned flour or egg and crumbs.
5. Fry steadily in hot butter and oil until crisp and golden brown.
6. Put on to skewers, top with a little cheese and put a slice of cheese between each ball.
7. Heat under the grill until the cheese has melted. Serve at once — in the picture the balls are served on cooked cabbage leaves to set off their colour. A crisp green salad is an excellent accompaniment.

Variation
The cheese may be omitted and the balls fried, then poached in well seasoned stock.

Argentinian ninos envueltos

Cooking time: 1½ hours
Preparation time: 30 minutes
Main cooking utensils: 1 or 2 saucepans (1 with lid)
Serves: 6

Imperial	Metric
1½ lb. beef topside or silverside, cut into 6 thin slices	¾ kg. beef topside or silverside, cut into 6 thin slices
seasoning	seasoning
Stuffing:	*Stuffing:*
1 medium-sized onion	1 medium-sized onion
2 oz. butter or margarine	50 g. butter or margarine
3 oz. soft white breadcrumbs	75 g. soft white breadcrumbs
1 oz. Parmesan cheese, grated	25 g. Parmesan cheese, grated
1 tablespoon chopped parsley	1 tablespoon chopped parsley
2 tablespoons finely chopped celery (optional)	2 tablespoons finely chopped celery (optional)
1 egg	1 egg
seasoning	seasoning
Sauce:	*Sauce:*
2 onions	2 onions
4 tablespoons oil	4 tablespoons oil
4 large tomatoes	4 large tomatoes
½ pint beef stock or water and 1 beef stock cube	300 ml. beef stock or water and 1 beef stock cube
¼ pint red wine	150 ml. red wine
2 bay leaves	2 bay leaves

1. Chop the onion for the stuffing and fry for a few minutes in the hot butter or margarine.
2. Remove the pan from the heat and add all the other stuffing ingredients.
3. Lay the slices of beef on a board and season lightly, then roll with a rolling pin until paper thin.
4. Spread with the stuffing and roll firmly, secure with cotton.
5. Chop the onions for the sauce and fry in the oil for a few minutes.
6. Add the beef rolls and brown these in the onion and oil mixture.
7. Add the skinned chopped tomatoes, stock or water and stock cube, wine, bay leaves and seasoning.
8. Cover the pan and simmer for 1 hour until the meat is tender.
9. Lift the meat rolls on to a hot dish, boil the sauce until reduced in quantity. Pour the sauce over the rolls and serve with carrots, peas and creamed potatoes.

Variation
Use stewing steak and allow 2 hours cooking time.

Crème brûlée

Cooking time: 2 hours 10 minutes
Preparation time: 15 minutes
Main cooking utensils: saucepan, ovenproof dish or pie dish,
    steamer (optional)
Oven temperature: very cool (275–300°F., 140–150°C., Gas
    Mark 1–2)
Oven position: centre
Serves: 4

Imperial	Metric
4 oz. sugar	100 g. sugar
3 tablespoons water	3 tablespoons water
$\frac{1}{2}$ pint thick cream and $\frac{1}{2}$ pint milk or 1 pint thin cream	275 ml. thick cream and 275 ml. milk or 550 ml. thin cream
4 eggs or egg yolks	4 eggs or egg yolks
2 oz. blanched almonds	50 g. blanched almonds
2 tablespoons icing or brown sugar	2 tablespoons icing or brown sugar

1. Make a caramel from 3 oz. (75 g.) of the sugar and 3 tablespoons water.
2. Add to this $\frac{3}{4}$ pint (425 ml.) of the liquid.
3. Heat gently without boiling until the caramel is absorbed.
4. Pour on to the eggs or egg yolks.
5. Add the remaining 1 oz. (25 g.) sugar and $\frac{1}{4}$ pint (125 ml.) cream.
6. Cover the top of the basin with buttered paper and cook very slowly in a steamer for about 2 hours or stand the dish in another containing cold water and bake in a slow oven for about 2 hours.
7. Remove the paper.
8. Cover the top with nuts or make a line down the centre as shown in the picture.
9. Sprinkle over the sieved icing or brown sugar and brown under a hot grill. Serve cold, with cream.

Variation
It may be served hot, although the flavour is better when cold.

Scottish trifle

Cooking time: 15 minutes
Preparation time: 20 minutes
Main cooking utensils: saucepan, double saucepan
Serves: 6–8

Imperial	Metric
4 sponge cakes	4 sponge cakes
2–3 tablespoons raspberry jam or redcurrant jelly	2–3 tablespoons raspberry jam or redcurrant jelly
2 large macaroon biscuits	2 large macaroon biscuits
3 tablespoons water	3 tablespoons water
3–4 oz. castor sugar	75–100 g. castor sugar
4–5 tablespoons light sherry	4–5 tablespoons light sherry
2 oz. seedless raisins	50 g. seedless raisins
1–2 oz. blanched almonds	25–50 g. blanched almonds
2 eggs	2 eggs
2 egg yolks	2 egg yolks
1¼ pints milk	700 ml. milk
piece lemon rind	piece lemon rind
few drops vanilla essence	few drops vanilla essence
Decoration:	*Decoration:*
¼–½ pint thick cream	150–250 ml. thick cream
few ratafias	few ratafias
few blanched almonds	few blanched almonds
glacé cherries	glacé cherries

1. Split the sponge cakes and sandwich them with the jam or jelly.
2. Put them into the serving dish and add the macaroon biscuits, broken into pieces.
3. Heat the water and 2 oz. (50 g.) of the sugar over a low heat until the sugar has dissolved; add the sherry.
4. Spoon over the sponge cakes; sprinkle the raisins and coarsely chopped blanched almonds on top.
5. Meanwhile beat the eggs and egg yolks with the remaining sugar.
6. Add the warm milk, lemon rind and essence, pour into the top of the double saucepan over hot water and cook gently, stirring well, until the custard coats the back of the wooden spoon.
7. Cool slightly, remove the lemon rind then pour over the sponge cakes.
8. Allow to cool and decorate with the whipped cream, ratafias, almonds and glacé cherries. Serve chilled.

Variation
Use half whisky and half sherry (this gives a strong flavour that most children will not enjoy).

Crème d'ananas

Cooking time: 15 minutes
Preparation time: 20 minutes, plus time to set
Main cooking utensils: double saucepan, saucepan, 2-pint (1-litre) mould
Serves: 4–6

Imperial	Metric
3 egg yolks	3 egg yolks
2 oz. castor sugar	50 g. castor sugar
$\frac{1}{2}$ pint milk	275 ml. milk
$\frac{1}{2}$ oz. powdered gelatine	15 g. powdered gelatine
1 small can pineapple rings	1 small can pineapple rings
$\frac{1}{2}$ pint thick cream	275 ml. thick cream
2 egg whites (see note)	2 egg whites (see note)
Decoration:	*Decoration:*
little extra cream	little extra cream
angelica	angelica

1. Beat the egg yolks with 1 oz. (25 g.) sugar, add the warmed milk, pour into the top of the double saucepan and cook (stirring well) over hot but not boiling water until the custard gives a thick coating over the back of a wooden spoon.

2. Meanwhile put the gelatine into a basin.

3. Measure $\frac{1}{4}$ pint (125 ml.) syrup from the pineapple and add 2—3 tablespoons of this syrup to the gelatine.

4. Heat the remaining syrup in the pan, add the softened gelatine and stir until dissolved.

5. Whisk the hot gelatine mixture into the hot custard, allow to cool and begin to stiffen slightly.

6. Drain and chop all the remaining pineapple finely except for 2 rings.

7. Fold the pineapple and whipped cream into the gelatine mixture.

8. Whisk the egg whites until stiff, beat in the remaining sugar then fold into the pineapple mixture.

9. Spoon into a mould (rinsed in cold water), allow to set. Turn out and decorate with whipped cream, pineapple pieces and angelica.

Note: Egg whites will not whip satisfactorily if they are taken straight from the refrigerator; keep at room temperature for 1 hour before using.

You can use a bowl over a pan of hot water instead of a double saucepan.

Pineapple soufflé

Cooking time: 10–15 minutes heating only
Preparation time: 25 minutes
Main cooking utensils: 7- to 7½-inch (18- to 19-cm.) soufflé dish, buttered greaseproof paper, 2 basins over a saucepan of hot water, one small, one large
Serves: 6–8

Imperial	Metric
1 medium-sized can pineapple rings	1 medium-sized can pineapple rings
$\frac{1}{2}$ oz. powdered gelatine (1 envelope)	15 g. powdered gelatine (1 envelope)
2 tablespoons white wine or dry sherry	2 tablespoons white wine or dry sherry
4 very large or 5 standard eggs	4 very large or 5 standard eggs
3–4 oz. sugar	75–100 g. sugar
$\frac{1}{2}$ pint thick cream	275 ml. thick cream
Decoration:	*Decoration:*
$\frac{1}{4}$ pint thick cream	125 ml. thick cream
small piece angelica	small piece angelica
some of the pineapple	some of the pineapple

1. Prepare the soufflé dish by pinning a double band of buttered paper above the rim of the dish.

2. Strain the syrup from the fruit, you need $\frac{1}{4}$ pint plus 1 tablespoon (150 ml.).

3. Dissolve the gelatine in 3 tablespoons syrup in a basin over hot water until thick and creamy.

4. Separate eggs; beat yolks with sugar in a basin over hot water until thick and creamy.

5. Pour the gelatine liquid on to the egg mixture steadily, whisking vigorously.

6. Chop enough well-drained pineapple to give about 6 generous tablespoons, keep the remainder for decoration.

7. Add to the egg yolk mixture and allow to stiffen slightly.

8. Fold in the whipped cream, this should be stiff enough to hold a slight shape, but not quite as stiff as for piping.

9. Fold in the stiffly beaten egg whites.

10. Pour the mixture into the soufflé dish, allow to set and decorate as in the picture.

Melon stuffed with yoghurt and fruit

Preparation time: 15 minutes
Main utensil: mixing bowl
Serves: 6

Imperial	Metric
1 large cantaloup or other ripe melon	1 large canteloup or other ripe melon
1 large firm ripe pear	1 large firm ripe pear
1–2 firm ripe peaches	1–2 firm ripe peaches
1 banana	1 banana
lemon juice	lemon juice
8 oz. redcurrants	200 g. redcurrants
few grapes or cherries	few grapes or cherries
sugar to taste	sugar to taste
$\frac{1}{2}$ pint yoghurt	275 ml. yoghurt

1. Cut segments out of the melon as shown in the picture. To do this, insert the tip of a sharp knife at the top of the melon, cut down towards the centre, feeling the knife going right through to the middle of the melon. Make a second cut, so removing a triangle of the flesh.

2. Continue like this; it is advisable to mark out the portions lightly on the skin before cutting, so you have an even arrangement.

3. Remove the melon pulp from the portions, and put into a bowl.

4. Mix with the diced, peeled pear, peaches and banana and sprinkle with lemon juice to keep them a good colour.

5. Add the redcurrants, halved grapes or cherries and sugar to taste.

6. Scoop out the seeds from the bottom half of the melon and fill with sweetened yoghurt.

7. Pile the fruit on top. Serve very cold.

Note: Melon is served as a dessert in many tropical countries, and countries where the fruit is plentiful. For a simple sweet, chill the segments of melon and pour over a little white wine or sherry. Halved small melons may be filled with port or red or white wine and sugar.

Chestnut Mont Blanc

Cooking time: 20 minutes
Preparation time: 20 minutes
Main cooking utensils: saucepan, plain thin pipe and piping bag
Serves: 3–4

Imperial	Metric
1 lb. chestnuts	$\frac{1}{2}$ kg. chestnuts
2 oz. sugar	50 g. sugar
little vanilla essence or vanilla pod	little vanilla essence or vanilla pod
approximately 12 tablespoons water	approximately 12 tablespoons water
Decoration:	*Decoration:*
$\frac{1}{4}$–$\frac{1}{2}$ pint thick cream	150–250 ml. thick cream

1. Simmer the nuts in water for 10 minutes, skin them and then finish cooking them in a syrup made with the sugar, vanilla essence or pod and about 12 tablespoons of water.

2. If using a vanilla pod, it should be put into the water and sugar, removed, washed and it can then be used again.

3. Sieve the chestnuts, leaving one whole for decoration, and pipe thin threads of the purée to form a pyramid. Decorate with whipped cream, and a whole chestnut.

Variation

Use canned, unsweetened purée of chestnuts instead of cooking the nuts as above. Sieve the purée, add vanilla essence and sugar to taste, then proceed as above.

Baked Alaska

Cooking time: 3–5 minutes
Preparation time: 10 minutes, plus time to prepare the sponge or pastry
Main cooking utensil: ovenproof dish or board covered with foil
Oven temperature: very hot (475–500°F., 240–250°C., Gas Mark 9–10)
Oven position: just above centre
Serves: 6–8

Imperial	Metric
1 square or round of sponge or cooked pastry	1 square or round of sponge or cooked pastry
fruit	fruit
1–2 blocks ice cream	1–2 blocks ice cream
5 egg whites	5 egg whites
5–10 oz. castor sugar (see stage 5)	125–250 g. castor sugar (see stage 5)
Decoration:	*Decoration:*
few glacé cherries	few glacé cherries
angelica	angelica

1. Put the sponge or pastry into the dish or on to the board.
2. Top with the fruit; although some juice may be allowed to soak through a sponge, keep the fruit well-drained if using pastry.
3. The dessert is nicer if fresh fruit is mashed with sugar to give a more moist texture.
4. Put the ice cream on top of the fruit and sponge or pastry.
5. Whisk the egg whites until very stiff, gradually beat in half the sugar, then fold in the remainder. (The quantity of sugar may be varied according to personal taste – the sweet is just as successful with the smaller amount.)
6. Pile or pipe over the ice cream and sponge; it is essential to cover the sweet completely. Decorate.
7. Put into the oven until tipped with brown.

Note: This is much better served hot, although it can stand for up to 20 minutes without the ice cream melting.

Fresh cream ice and Macaroons

Cooking time: 20 minutes
Freezing time: 1–1½ hours
Preparation time: 20 minutes each
Main cooking utensils: freezing tray, baking tray
Oven temperature: very moderate (325–350°F., 170–180°C., Gas Mark 3–4)
Oven position: centre
Serves: 4

Fresh cream ice

Imperial
$\frac{1}{2}$ pint thick cream or $\frac{1}{4}$ pint
  thick and $\frac{1}{4}$ pint thin cream
2–3 oz. sieved icing sugar
$\frac{1}{4}$–$\frac{1}{2}$ teaspoon vanilla essence
2 egg whites
Decoration:
2–3 oz. chocolate vermicelli
  or grated chocolate

Metric
275 ml. thick cream or 150 ml.
  thick and 125 ml. thin cream
50–75 g. sieved icing sugar
$\frac{1}{4}$–$\frac{1}{2}$ teaspoon vanilla essence
2 egg whites
Decoration:
50–75 g. chocolate vermicelli
  or grated chocolate

1. Check the refrigerator manufacturer's instructions for freezing ice cream or turn the indicator on the refrigerator to the coldest setting 30 minutes in advance.
2. Whip the cream until it just holds its shape. If using all thick cream, be careful not to over-whip it.
3. Fold in the icing sugar and vanilla essence.
4. Whisk the egg whites until very stiff, and blend with the cream.
5. Freeze until quite firm. If wished the ice cream may be taken out of the freezing tray when nearly frozen, whipped well and then returned to the tray to freeze again. This tends to give a lighter texture, but in this recipe is not essential. Serve in glasses, decorated with chocolate, with the macaroons.

Macaroons

Imperial
2 egg whites
few drops almond essence
4 oz. ground almonds
4 oz. sugar
rice paper (optional)
Filling:
2 oz. butter mixed with
  4 oz. melted chocolate

Metric
2 egg whites
few drops almond essence
100 g. ground almonds
100 g. sugar
rice paper (optional)
Filling:
50 g. butter mixed with
  100 g. melted chocolate

1. Whisk the egg whites lightly, add the essence, ground almonds and sugar.
2. Form into small balls, put on to rice paper or a well greased baking tray and bake until golden. Cool and sandwich with the chocolate cream.

Pears and ice cream with chocolate sauce

Cooking time: few minutes
Preparation time: 10 minutes
Main cooking utensil: basin and saucepan or double saucepan
Serves: 4

Imperial	Metric
4 medium-sized ripe pears	4 medium-sized ripe pears
lemon juice	lemon juice
block vanilla ice cream	block vanilla ice cream
Sauce:	*Sauce:*
6 oz. plain chocolate	150 g. plain chocolate
few drops vanilla essence	few drops vanilla essence
1 oz. butter	25 g. butter
2 tablespoons water	2 tablespoons water
1 oz. castor sugar	25 g. castor sugar
2 teaspoons golden syrup	2 teaspoons golden syrup
Decoration:	*Decoration:*
chocolate curls	chocolate curls

1. To make the sauce, chop the chocolate into small pieces and put it into a basin or the top of a double saucepan with the other ingredients; if serving the sauce cold use double the amount of water as the sauce thickens as it cools.

2. Melt over hot, but not boiling water; if the water is too hot the sauce loses its shine and becomes hard, rather than melting.

3. Peel, halve and core the pears.

4. Sprinkle with lemon juice and cover, if allowing to stand, to keep the colour.

5. Spoon the ice cream into glasses with the pears then top with the hot or cold chocolate sauce.

6. Decorate with curls of chocolate. To make these scrape along a block of chocolate with a sharp knife and the thin wafers of chocolate will curl. For large curls, melt the chocolate, pour on to a tin and leave to set, then proceed as above. Serve with wafers.

Variation
Use home-made ice cream (see page 109).

Moka sauce: Use strong coffee instead of water for the sauce.

Sorbets

Cooking time: 10 minutes
Preparation time: 15 minutes
Main cooking utensils: saucepan, strainer, freezing tray
Serves: 4–6

Imperial	Metric
Orange sorbet:	*Orange sorbet:*
5–6 large oranges	5–6 large oranges
1 lemon	1 lemon
$\frac{1}{2}$ pint water	275 ml. water
3–4 oz. sugar	75–100 g. sugar
2 egg whites	2 egg whites
Lemon sorbet:	*Lemon sorbet:*
4 large lemons	4 large lemons
$\frac{1}{2}$ pint water	275 ml. water
4–5 oz. sugar	100–125 g. sugar
2 egg whites	2 egg whites

1. Squeeze out the juice from the fruit.
2. Remove any pith from the skins and put the skins with the water into a pan and simmer steadily.
3. Strain carefully to give a clear liquid, add the sugar while hot, stir to dissolve, then add the syrup to the fruit juice.
4. Taste and, if necessary, add more sugar to give a sweeter flavour – remember freezing reduces sweetness slightly; never over-sweeten.
5. Put into the freezing tray, freeze for approximately 30 minutes in the freezing compartment.
6. Whisk the egg whites until stiff, add the partially frozen mixture and fold together.
7. Return to the refrigerator and leave until firm – 45 minutes to 1 hour. In a home freezer the time will be shorter.
8. Serve with whipped cream if liked.

Crêpes Suzette

Cooking time: few minutes for each pancake
Preparation time: 20 minutes
Main cooking utensils: saucepan, frying pan
Serves: 4

Imperial	Metric
Pancakes:	*Pancakes:*
4 oz. plain flour	100 g. plain flour
pinch salt	pinch salt
1 oz. sugar	25 g. sugar
2 eggs	2 eggs
barely ½ pint milk or milk and water	250 ml. milk or milk and water
2 oz. butter	50 g. butter
To fry:	*To fry:*
olive oil	olive oil
Filling:	*Filling:*
3 oz. butter	75 g. butter
3 oz. sugar	75 g. sugar
2 oranges	2 oranges
1 lemon	1 lemon
2 tablespoons rose jam or redcurrant jelly	2 tablespoons rose jam or redcurrant jelly
2 tablespoons orange marmalade	2 tablespoons orange marmalade
Syrup:	*Syrup:*
approximately 4 tablespoons orange liqueur	approximately 4 tablespoons orange liqueur
approximately 4 tablespoons brandy	approximately 4 tablespoons brandy

1. Sieve the flour and salt into a bowl, add the sugar.
2. Gradually beat in the eggs, then the milk, to give a soft batter.
3. Heat the butter, allow to cool slightly, whisk into the batter.
4. Heat a little oil in the pan, fry the pancakes on the underside until golden, toss or turn, cook on the second side.
5. Lift each pancake out of the pan and put on a plate, heat a little extra olive oil before frying the next. Continue until all the batter is used (makes 8–10 pancakes).
6. Cream the butter and sugar, add the grated fruit rind and 4 tablespoons juice, then the jam or jelly and marmalade.
7. Spread the mixture on each pancake, roll or fold in four.
8. Heat enough orange liqueur and brandy to cover the bottom of the pan, add as many pancakes as can be fitted in. Heat.
9. Ignite the liqueur in the pan, serve at once. Continue like this until all the pancakes have been heated. Serve with cream.

Californian prune flan

Cooking time: 30 minutes
Preparation time: 30 minutes plus time for dough to chill
Main cooking utensils: 8- to 9-inch (20- to 23-cm.) sandwich tin
Oven temperature: hot (425—450°F., 220—230°C., Gas Mark 7—8)
   then moderate (375°F., 190°C., Gas Mark 5)
Serves: 5—6

Imperial	Metric
9 oz. plain flour	225 g. plain flour
4½ oz. unsalted butter	115 g. unsalted butter
1½ oz. sugar	40 g. sugar
grated rind and juice of 1 lemon	grated rind and juice of 1 lemon
2 egg yolks	2 egg yolks
few drops vanilla essence	few drops vanilla essence
water to mix	water to mix
Filling:	*Filling:*
6 oz. well-drained cooked stoned prunes	150 g. well-drained cooked stoned prunes
8 cooked or drained canned apricots	8 cooked or drained canned apricots
1 tablespoon sugar	1 tablespoon sugar
2 teaspoons lemon juice	2 teaspoons lemon juice

1. Sieve the flour and rub in the butter until mixture resembles fine breadcrumbs.
2. Add the sugar and lemon rind, then bind with the lemon juice, egg yolks, vanilla essence and enough water to make a soft dough.
3. Knead lightly on a floured board (the dough will be much stickier to handle than pastry) and press into the greased sandwich tin. If the dough is rather soft to handle leave it in a cool place for about 30 minutes before kneading.
4. Chill the dough in the tin for 30 minutes.
5. Fill the flan with the prunes and apricots, sprinkle with sugar and lemon juice and bake in a hot oven for 15 minutes.
6. Lower heat to moderate and bake for a further 15 minutes or until firm and golden. Serve hot or cold.

Note: The prunes shown in the picture are the stoned type which are tenderised and therefore do not need soaking before cooking.

Grape tart

Cooking time: 45 minutes
Preparation time: 15 minutes
Main cooking utensils: large shallow saucepan, ovenproof dish
Oven temperature: moderate (350–375°F., 180–190°C., Gas Mark 4–5)
Oven position: centre
Serves: 4–6

Imperial	Metric
12 oz. grapes (preferably black)	300 g. grapes (preferably black)
3 oz. sugar	75 g. sugar
$\frac{1}{4}$ pint white wine or water	125 ml. white wine or water
Batter:	*Batter:*
2 oz. butter	50 g. butter
4 oz. sugar	100 g. sugar
2 large eggs	2 large eggs
6 oz. flour (plain or self-raising)	150 g. flour (plain or self-raising)
12 tablespoons milk	12 tablespoons milk
To serve:	*To serve:*
sugar or vanilla sugar (see note)	sugar or vanilla sugar (see note)

1. Remove the seeds from the grapes, but keep grapes whole and do not skin them.

2. Make a syrup with the sugar and liquid, bring this to the boil.

3. Put in the grapes, simmer gently for a few minutes, then lift out.

4. To make the batter, cream the butter well, add the sugar and beat again, then add the beaten eggs.

5. Stir in the flour and milk to give a smooth, thick batter.

6. Blend the well-drained grapes with this.

7. Put into a well-greased baking dish and cook until just firm.

8. Towards the end of cooking time, it may be necessary to cover the top to prevent the fruit drying. Serve cold, topped with plenty of sugar; equally good as a dessert or for tea.

Note: Vanilla sugar is made by putting half a vanilla pod into a jar of sugar. The sugar gradually absorbs the flavour.

Variation

Use other fruit, and use less batter — i.e., 1$\frac{1}{2}$ lb. ($\frac{3}{4}$ kg.) fruit and half the ingredients for the batter — this makes it more suitable for a hot dessert.

Raspberry-filled choux

Cooking time: 25 minutes
Preparation time: 30 minutes
Main cooking utensils: 2 saucepans, baking trays
Oven temperature: hot (425–450°F., 220–230°C., Gas Mark 7–8)
   then moderate (375°F., 190°C., Gas Mark 5)
Oven position: just above centre
Makes: 8 choux

Imperial	Metric
Pastry:	*Pastry:*
¼ pint water	125 ml. water
1½ oz. butter	40 g. butter
3 oz. flour	75 g. flour
2 medium eggs	2 medium eggs
1 egg yolk	1 egg yolk
Confectioner's custard:	*Confectioner's custard:*
1 level tablespoon cornflour	1 level tablespoon cornflour
½ pint milk	275 ml. milk
2 teaspoons sugar	2 teaspoons sugar
few drops vanilla essence or vanilla sugar	few drops vanilla essence or vanilla sugar
2 egg yolks	2 egg yolks
¼ pint thick cream	125 ml. thick cream
Filling:	*Filling:*
1–1¼ lb. raspberries	approximately ½ kg. raspberries

1. To make the pastry, put the water and butter into a saucepan and heat until the butter has dissolved. Remove from the heat and stir in the flour.

2. Cook over a gentle heat, stirring well until the mixture forms into a dry ball.

3. Remove from the heat again and gradually beat in the eggs and egg yolk until the texture becomes smooth and sticky.

4. Pile or pipe into 8 rounds on a greased tray.

5. Cook for about 20 minutes in a hot oven, then lower heat to crisp the pastry.

6. Allow to cool, cut off the tops and remove the sticky inside.

7. Blend the cornflour with the milk, cook until thickened and smooth, add the sugar, vanilla and egg yolks, continue cooking without boiling until very thick.

8. Cool, stirring well, then fold in the whipped cream.

9. Fill the choux with most of the confectioner's custard and fruit. Top with the lids and a spoonful of custard. Serve any remaining fruit round the choux.

Strawberry cake

Cooking time: 35 minutes
Preparation time: 25 minutes
Main cooking utensils: 2 8-inch (20-cm.) sandwich tins, greaseproof
   paper
Oven temperature: moderate (350–375°F., 180–190°C., Gas Mark
   4 5)
Oven position: centre
Makes: 8–10 servings

Imperial	**Metric**
4 oz. ground almonds	100 g. ground almonds
5 egg whites	5 egg whites
9 oz. castor sugar	275 g. castor sugar
½ teaspoon vanilla essence	½ teaspoon vanilla essence
1 teaspoon lemon juice	1 teaspoon lemon juice
2 teaspoons hot water	2 teaspoons hot water
Filling:	*Filling:*
½ pint thick cream	275 ml. thick cream
½ teaspoon vanilla essence	½ teaspoon vanilla essence
little sugar	little sugar
1–1½ lb. strawberries (preferably wild)	1–1½ lb. strawberries (preferably wild)
little Kirsch	little Kirsch

1. Spread the almonds on a tin and brown for about 5 minutes in the oven; cool.
2. Whisk the egg whites until very stiff.
3. Gradually beat in half the sugar, fold in the remainder.
4. Fold in the almonds, vanilla essence, lemon juice and water.
5. Line the bottom of the tins with greaseproof paper.
6. Grease the paper and sides well.
7. Put in almond mixture — do not level if a slightly uneven texture is required as in the picture.
8. Bake until firm. Turn out and peel off the paper.
9. Whip the cream, add the vanilla essence.
10. Sweeten the strawberries and flavour with Kirsch. Sandwich the cooled cake with cream and fruit.

Kerstkransjes

Cooking time: 10–12 minutes
Preparation time: 15–20 minutes plus time to chill
Main cooking utensils: baking trays
Oven temperature: moderate to moderately hot (350–375°F.,
    180–190°C., Gas Mark 4–5)
Oven position: just above centre
Makes: 30 biscuits

Imperial	Metric
5 oz. plain flour	125 g. plain flour
2 oz. sieved icing sugar	50 g. sieved icing sugar
pinch salt	pinch salt
4 oz. butter	100 g. butter
$\frac{1}{2}$–1 teaspoon vanilla essence	$\frac{1}{2}$–1 teaspoon vanilla essence
egg to bind	egg to bind
Glaze:	*Glaze:*
1 egg (if necessary, see stage 3)	1 egg (if necessary, see stage 3)
1 oz. finely chopped blanched almonds	25 g. finely chopped blanched almonds
1 oz. granulated sugar	25 g. granulated sugar

1. Sieve the flour, icing sugar and salt together.

2. Cream the butter with the vanilla essence.

3. Work in the flour mixture, knead very well, then add sufficient egg to bind. You may find you have enough egg for the glaze.

4. Wrap the mixture in foil or greaseproof paper and chill for an hour; it helps to chill the mixture more rapidly if you divide it into two or three portions and chill these separately.

5. Roll out to about $\frac{1}{8}$ inch ($\frac{1}{4}$ cm.) in thickness.

6. Cut into circles about $2\frac{1}{2}$ inches (6 cm.) in diameter.

7. Remove the centres with a 1-inch ($2\frac{1}{2}$-cm.) cutter.

8. Gather up the dough removed, knead lightly and roll out as stages 5, 6 and 7.

9. Brush the rings with beaten egg and top with the almonds and sugar.

10. Lift on to ungreased trays and bake in a moderate to moderately hot oven until golden brown.

11. Cool on the baking trays, then store in an airtight tin.

Punch marquise and Le brulo

Preparation time: 10 minutes
Main cooking utensil: saucepan
Serves: 8 (each punch)

Punch marquise

Imperial
1 lemon
1 bottle sweet or medium-sweet
  white wine (Sauternes,
  Entre-deux-Mers, Graves)
4 oz. sugar (depending on
  wine used)
1–2 cloves
small piece cinnamon stick
$\frac{1}{4}$–$\frac{1}{2}$ pint brandy, depending
  upon personal taste
Decoration:
1 seedless lemon

Metric
1 lemon
1 bottle sweet or medium-sweet
  white wine (Sauternes,
  Entre-deux-Mers, Graves)
100 g. sugar (depending on
  wine used)
1–2 cloves
small piece cinnamon stick
150–250 ml. brandy, depending
  upon personal taste
Decoration:
1 seedless lemon

1. Pare the rind from the lemon, discarding the white pith, which could make the drink bitter.
2. Put the wine, sugar, lemon rind and spices into a saucepan and heat until boiling point is reached — do not allow to continue boiling.
3. Strain into a hot bowl.
4. Add the brandy, heated in the pan for 1–2 minutes, then ignite the drink.
5. Leave for 1–2 minutes, when the flame will doubtless have burnt itself out. Top with slices of lemon.

Variation
Add $\frac{1}{4}$ pint (125 ml.) moderately strong, very well-strained tea to the wine.

Le brulo

Imperial
4 large oranges
8–16 lumps sugar
8 measures of brandy

Metric
4 large oranges
8–16 lumps sugar
8 measures of brandy

1. Halve the oranges and remove the pulp (this can be used in a fruit salad).
2. Put the sugar into the cases and crush against the sides of the oranges.
3. Add the brandy, ignite this, then pour the orange-flavoured drink into warmed brandy glasses. The brandy takes on a most interesting flavour when ignited in this way.

Acknowledgements

The following photographs are by courtesy of:

Argentine Beef Bureau: page 92
Armour: page 50
Californian Prune Advisory Bureau: page 68
Dutch Dairy Bureau: pages 30, 48, 124
Dutch Fruit and Vegetable Producers' Association: pages 102, 120
Fruit Producers' Council: pages 46, 110
H.P. Sauce: page 14
Karl Ostmann, Limited (Germany): page 52
Lawry's Foods International Incorporated: page 8
Libby McNeill and Libby Limited: page 12
Sunsweet Prunes: page 116
Tate and Lyle Limited: page 122
The Friends of Wine: page 126